# SOCIAL ANXIETY AS A TEEN

DISCOVER 5 PRACTICAL WAYS TO OVERCOME THIS DISORDER BY CHALLENGING YOUR PERSONAL BEHAVIORS, REFRAMING NEGATIVE THOUGHTS, AND FINDING RELIEF IN LIVING LIFE TO THE FULLEST.

### NATASHA RAE SIMMONS

© **Copyright 2023 - All rights reserved.**

The content contained within this book may not be reproduced, duplicated, or transmitted without direct written permission from the author or the publisher.

Under no circumstances will any blame or legal responsibility be held against the publisher, or author, for any damages, reparation, or monetary loss due to the information contained within this book. Either directly or indirectly. You are responsible for your own choices, actions, and results.

**Legal Notice:**

This book is copyright protected. This book is only for personal use. You cannot amend, distribute, sell, use, quote, or paraphrase any part, or the content within this book, without the consent of the author or publisher.

**Disclaimer Notice:**

Please note the information contained within this document is for educational and entertainment purposes only. All effort has been executed to present accurate, up-to-date, and reliable, complete information. No warranties of any kind are declared or implied. Readers acknowledge that the author is not engaging in the rendering of legal, financial, medical, or professional advice. The content within this book has been derived from various sources. Please consult a licensed professional before attempting any techniques outlined in this book.

By reading this document, the reader agrees that under no circumstances is the author responsible for any losses, direct or indirect, which are incurred as a result of the use of the information contained within this document, including, but not limited to, — errors, omissions, or inaccuracies.

# TABLE OF CONTENTS

| | |
|---|---|
| Introduction | v |
| 1. What is Social Anxiety? | 1 |
| 2. The Symptoms, Root Causes, and Identifying Factors | 13 |
| 3. The Effects of Social Anxiety | 49 |
| 4. Challenge Your Personal Behaviors | 57 |
| 5. Choose Change for Your Thoughts | 81 |
| 6. Practical Tips | 94 |
| 7. Application in Your Current Situation | 116 |
| 8. Living Life to The Fullest | 154 |
| Conclusion | 175 |
| References | 179 |

# INTRODUCTION

If I may ask, with the utmost respect, why did you decide on this book? Is it because you are scared of something—maybe, social interactions, public speaking, talking to strangers, criticism, or looking people in the eye? Well, what if I told you that fear is a normal, natural part of being human? Fear keeps you alive. It's the reason we don't jump from tall buildings or in front of moving trains. But fear is a complex emotion that can take many forms, social anxiety being one of the most powerful, crippling ones. Social anxiety, as isolating and lonely as it may feel, is more common than you think. Most teens struggle with social anxiety, and up to 25% struggle so severely that they need medical intervention. This is to say that, statistically, one of every four teenagers

## INTRODUCTION

you meet relates to your pain and struggles or has it worse.[1]

It sucks to think of just how much power anxiety has over your life. You often feel out of place. More like an outcast looking at the world from the outside instead of living in it. You feel anxious around people and question whether they like you or not. Sometimes, you are convinced they don't. You wonder if they think you are strange, odd, or weird; you often think they do. You are too scared to go out to a party or do a presentation in class because the thought of being the center of attention, even for a few minutes, scares you witless.

And while you slowly shrink deeper into the dark hole that threatens to consume you, everyone around you seems happy and content. They are living their best lives, have perfect skin, have the coolest partners, have no problem expressing themselves, and do everything they've always wanted. It's so easy to be envious of such people. You may compare yourself with the "cool" kids and other famous influencers who seem to have it all together. You may even wish that you were them or like them. Surely, they must be living their best lives; they are floating and breezing through life with no care in the world. They don't look like they struggle

## INTRODUCTION

at all. No one, but you, is trapped in their own minds.

In reality, even people who seem like they have it all figured out, deal with their fair share of struggles. They have insecurities, fears, and challenges. The only variance between you and them is that they are good at dealing with these struggles or masking them altogether. They are fierce and have mastered the art of hiding their flaws and controlling other people's perceptions of who they are.

Social anxiety makes you question yourself, your sense of self-worth, self-confidence, and self-esteem. You'll find yourself doubting your abilities, appearance, relationships, and even your sanity. And that's not as bad as it gets; the extra cherry on top is that anxiety can easily distort your sense of reality and your ability to see and analyze situations objectively. When it flares up, it may cripple your ability to read people and situations and can be the reason why the blow-up is happening in the first place. This typically occurs when anxiety has a firm grip on you physically, mentally, emotionally, and behaviorally.

I mentioned earlier that anxiety is complex. It's like a spectrum that affects everyone differently. If you were to meet ten teens right now, they'd all describe different ways anxiety affects them. That's

## INTRODUCTION

because each of us has different triggers. Maybe some of the examples described above don't apply to you. Some may bother you, and others don't. Maybe you experience anxiety in social settings, on your way to the doctor, school, in new surroundings—or just out of the blue. For another teen, it could come in the form of physical symptoms such as dizziness, nausea, shortness of breath, sweating, tingling, or an increased heart rate. Still, others may struggle with anxiety in their mind, manifesting as negative or racing thoughts, brain freeze, or beehive brain buzz. Sadly, most of these symptoms don't always happen as independently as I've described above. It's often a mix of many symptoms, such as negative thoughts, a racing heart, and dizziness when it strikes.

If any of these sound familiar, you'll want to try the five practical tips designed to help teens overcome the anxiety described in this book. Why do you wonder? Well, the strategies I've shared in this book helped me overcome my own social challenges. I, just like you, struggled a lot with social anxiety as a teen; I felt like an outcast or that I didn't fit in for the longest time. I struggled with relationships and didn't know how to make or keep friends. Like many teens, I was always worried about my studies and what the future held for me. I was scared to be around teachers or my classmates. After many years of struggling to build meaningful connections and constantly feeling frozen in fear whenever the spotlight shone on me, I realized this was no way to live. I had finally reached my breaking point, and I wanted to change things. I asked myself tough questions, "*Is this all there is to life—living in constant fear and anxiety? Could I be the one standing in my way of living my best life? What if the person holding me back was no one but myself?*"

As I asked myself these questions and answered them as honestly as possible, I realized I had a choice. I had it in me to change my circumstances and pull myself out of my current situation. I realized the wall I had put up wasn't protective. No! It was just a barrier, limiting my potential and keeping me from making friends or taking action. I decided that I wanted to break through my anxiety once and for all. I was sick and tired of feeling inadequate or like I wasn't good enough. I was done with fear and having to worry about what others thought of me. I was ready to break out of my shell, but I knew I'd have to work through it.

I bet you've also asked yourself some if not all, these questions. You've wondered if there's a way to boost your confidence and overcome anxiety. Maybe

## INTRODUCTION

you've always wanted to scale up your game, like all the confident teens you see at school or on social media, but don't know where to start. Maybe you've been more hung up on trying to get by without embarrassing yourself in front of others, but now you are ready to break through all your issues.

Fantastic!

I wrote this book with one and only one goal in mind; to help you overcome social anxiety by challenging your behaviors, reframing negative thoughts, and showing you how to find relief in living life to the fullest. After combing through and studying my own life experiences and years of thorough and extensive research on this subject, I came up with a list of practical exercises that have been proven to help teens with their anxiety. I'm excited to share everything with you. I will lay out and explain, in great detail, five of the most powerful and practical techniques for coping with and overcoming social anxiety that I've learned over the years.

Everyone's journey to confidence starts with the belief that it's possible. I want you to believe that it is possible because it is, and you have a way out; you can break free. Yes, it may take a while and may require some effort. At some point, you may find yourself coming face-to-face with the same things

## INTRODUCTION

that scare you, but after all these, you'll come out as a winner. You'll make it to the other side as a new person, a happy teen, comfortable in their own skin.

Before you start, you must understand your situation. If you were to go to a doctor today with strange symptoms, does the doctor prescribe the medication first, or do they try to understand your symptoms first? The same applies here. It would help if you first went through the journey of self-discovery to understand what you should be working on. Understanding what causes your anxiety, fears, and insecurities will help you find healing sooner. This is the first step toward overcoming your challenges. If you, at any point, feel overwhelmed, remember it's okay. Take a break; take 10, then keep going. I'd like you to challenge yourself. I want you to try; you have everything to gain and nothing to lose in trying.

If you are ready to break loose and overcome your anxiety, turn the pages.

# CHAPTER 1
# WHAT IS SOCIAL ANXIETY?

Every second of every day, life is like this. Anxiety. Fear. Apprehension. Fear of being judged. Worry about what you may have said or done wrong. Fear about how you look. Intense worry about other people's rejection and disapproval. Scared of rejection. Fear about not fitting in, not being as confident and cool as everyone else. Too self-conscious to start a conversation; scared that you'll say something embarrassing or have nothing important to add to the conversation. You try your best to cover and mask your perceived flaws. You are living, daily, the torture and chronic pain of something called social anxiety also referred to as social phobia. These chains have taken over your life, and they have a firm grip on you.

Indeed, most, if not all, of us are familiar with the

nervous and uncomfortable feelings associated with being around certain social situations. Consider this: maybe you felt extremely embarrassed when you met someone for the first time, felt nervous going on a first date with someone you liked, or got butterflies in your stomach when you made that big presentation at school. We all know how awkward it is to walk into a room full of strangers. Public speaking isn't as exciting as it sounds, either. We've all been there. But social anxiety is different. It cripples you completely so that instead of being scared of a room full of people and walking into it anyway, you avoid the room or the occasion altogether. Social phobia makes you "crawl inside your shell" to protect yourself from situations that make you uncomfortable.

    The stress of being in social settings overwhelms you; it's just too much to handle when dealing with social phobia. In that case, normal situations cause you great stress and embarrassment. You are constantly and highly self-conscious about how you look, what you are wearing, what people think of you, whether they like you or not, and whether you said, looked, or sounded stupid or not. Many people who struggle with social phobia are extremely self-aware, always looking for reasons to think others are judging and scrutinizing them. When social anxiety takes over your life, it wreaks havoc not only on your social life but also on other areas of your life. Ultimately, the extreme stress and self-awareness spill over and affect your schooling, relationships with friends and loved ones, daily routines, and work. You may find yourself avoiding all social contact for reasons that may seem small to others—for example, small talk makes you uncomfortable, or meeting strangers makes you sick. And research shows that unchecked social anxiety could become a long-term, chronic health condition.[1]

While socially anxious people are scared of certain situations for different reasons, many dread social interactions due to their acute fear of:

- Offending someone unintentionally.
- Being watched by people around, which is often the case when they are at the center of attention.
- Being embarrassed and humiliated by themselves or others around them.

## WHAT CAUSES SOCIAL ANXIETY DISORDER?

Social anxiety disorder is an extreme reaction to things that aren't as dangerous as someone suffering from it thinks it is. Still, the body reacts like the danger is real and extreme. This means that someone struggling with social phobia feels real sensations of fear which is part of the body's natural fight and flight response. This response happens naturally when we are scared. It is an autonomic nervous system response that alerts our brains to the dangers around us so we can protect ourselves. With a social anxiety disorder, this "alarm" is activated too frequently, too strongly, and in irrelevant situations. But, as you can recall, the body's responses are real because the brain doesn't differentiate between real and perceived threats; to it, a threat is a threat, and therefore, even perceived threats seem real. Accordingly, the person reacts the same way they would in real danger—they freeze up, are completely paralyzed, and cannot interact with others.

People with social anxiety interpret these physical responses and emotions by avoiding the situation, *"Oh, my heart is racing, and I'm sweating. This must be dangerous. I better get out of here."* Someone else who doesn't have a social phobia will interpret the situation differently, "*Okay, that's just my heart pounding. That is me getting nervous because I'm about to go up and speak. It's no big deal, it happens, but I can deal with it.*"

## WHAT IS SOCIAL ANXIETY?

Consider the following scenarios.

An eighteen-year-old girl finds walking a few blocks to the grocery shop around the corner extremely hard. She is highly self-conscious and scared that people are watching her from their windows. To add insult to injury, there's always a chance she'll run into a neighbor on the sidewalk, and she may be forced to greet them and entertain small talk. She doubts she can do that. She is petrified that her "hello" will sound weak, and the neighbor may see that she is terrified. This is the worst part because she doesn't want anybody to know she is scared. She tries her best to keep her eyes safely away from anyone she meets and hopes she doesn't have to talk to anybody.

Another person is sick of the line at the grocery store because it gives strangers a chance to look and stare at them. Deep down, they understand that it might not be true, but they can't shake off that feeling. As they shop, they are worried and extremely conscious that someone is watching them from the mirrors inside the ceiling. Now they must talk to the cashier who's checking out their items. They try to smile and say hi but can't get the words out. Soon enough, their anxiety goes through the roof, and they feel like they are embarrassing and making a fool of themselves. A man is sitting at his desk, staring at the telephone. He is in agony because he's too scared to pick up the phone and make an important phone call. He is afraid of calling an unknown person about a business deal because he fears rejection or making them angry. He doesn't know who will pick up, and the person doesn't know him either, but he is scared of being rejected, even though it's over the phone and they've never met. Even when he knows the person, he is often too scared that he could be calling at the wrong time and the other person could be busy, and this could make them angry, and they won't want anything to do with the phone call. He is entertaining feelings of rejection, even though he hasn't made the call yet. Eventually, he musters enough courage to make the call. Still, when it's over, he sits, analyzing and ruminating over everything that was said, the tone it was said in, and how the other person perceived them. His anxiety-racing thoughts convince him that he "messed up" the call, "just like he always does." He gets embarrassed just thinking about the call he just made.

Another young man has been invited to a party by his new neighbor. He wants to go because he feels

## WHAT IS SOCIAL ANXIETY?

exceptionally lonely, but he is too scared to go anywhere because he doesn't want to meet new people. He imagines how many people will be at the party—he concludes that there will be too many. He hates this because he knows the crowd will make him feel uncomfortable. He is scared of the mere thought of meeting and introducing himself to new people. Maybe he won't know what to say. Maybe they'll stare at him and make him feel unworthy. Maybe they'll reject him outright. Even if they act friendly and kind, they may notice his frozen look and inability to express himself or fully smile. They'll know he is uncomfortable, tense, and scared, and perhaps they'll not like this. No matter how he looks at it, he can never win. "I'm never going to fit in," he says. And he stays home again that night, alone, sad, and with the television as his only company. Home is the only place he feels comfortable and accepted. In fact, he hasn't been out for years. Besides, he doesn't have any friends or a strong network of support that could help him overcome his social phobia.

A freshman knows he won't attend classes on the first day of school because he is sure the professor will ask everyone in the class to introduce themselves. The simple thought of just sitting there and having to introduce himself in a room full of strangers looking at him, with him being the center of attention, at least for those few seconds, makes him sick. He knows his mind will be foggy, he will start trembling, and he may even forget important details. Maybe he'll say something stupid, his voice will shake, and he will sound scared and tense; everyone will see through him, then they'll laugh at him, and he'll be completely embarrassed. These thoughts overwhelm him, and he decides he better not show up. This way, he can avoid the responsibility of having to introduce himself to strangers.

These scenarios summarize some of the most common ways social phobia affects people. The symptoms manifest uniquely in each of us.

## THE IMPACT OF ANXIETY ON YOUR LIFE

Social phobia stands in your way of living your life to the fullest. While many people may consider certain situations normal, like school and work, you'll find excuses to avoid them. You'll also likely wonder how everyone around you looks okay and can easily handle themselves in social settings. This way, social anxiety could lead to:

# WHAT IS SOCIAL ANXIETY?

- Low self-esteem and self-worth.
- Negative thought patterns.
- Depression.
- Extreme and unhealthy sensitivity to criticism.
- Difficulty having and maintaining relationships.
- Low social skills.
- Isolation and trouble making friends.
- Low academic performance.
- Substance and drug abuse.
- Suicidal thoughts, attempts, and self-harm.

## HOW SOCIAL ANXIETY CAN AFFECT A TEEN'S LIFE

Social phobia leads to extreme self-consciousness and shyness, often spiraling into intense fear. As a result, a teen who has social phobia will avoid what others would consider everyday situations. Indeed, people with social anxiety disorder can interact normally and freely with friends and family. Still, they hate meeting new people and never talk in groups or in public because their self-consciousness takes over. Their fears get in the way of life, so instead of enjoying themselves, they dread social interactions. As a teen suffering from a social anxiety disorder, your fears about how others perceive you are extremely exaggerated in your mind. You focus more on embarrassing and humiliating things that could happen instead of the positive things. By doing this, a situation seems worse than it is.

Social anxiety disorder can lead to loneliness and disappointment over missed opportunities for social interactions, building friendships, and having fun. You may never ask someone you like out on a date, go to a party, join an after-school club, or chat with friends during breaks. If this is the case, how will you make or maintain friendships? Friendships thrive through communication and interactions. For this reason, you may struggle with loneliness and isolation.

You may not get the most out of school. Because you are too scared of drawing any attention towards yourself, you'll never answer a question in class, read out loud for others to hear, or give a presentation. You'll be too nervous to ask your teacher or classmates for help or even ask questions when you need help understanding something. Ultimately, you'll miss great opportunities to share your skills and talents with others and learn new skills. Since you struggle with self-consciousness, you may never gather enough courage to audition for a school play or talent show or join a team, club, or service project. You'll be too scared to try new things and make mistakes that could teach you and help you polish your skills.

## SOCIAL ANXIETY AFFECTS PEOPLE OF ALL AGES

You aren't alone in this either because studies show that social phobia is one of the most frequently occurring mental health illnesses. The National Institute of Mental Health (NIMH) recently reported that 19.1% of adults in the United States alone struggled with social anxiety in the last twelve months. The same study showed that lifetime rates are even more alarming, with over 31.1% of the population dealing with different forms of anxiety. Still, social anxiety is less common in older adults but relatively common in teens. NIMH reports that social anxiety impacts a whopping 32.3% of teens aged 17-18, 32.1% of teens aged 15-16, and another 31.4% of teens aged 13-14. You'd be intrigued to learn also that social anxiety could start as early as 11 years old, stretching all the way to 19 years old. These percentages could translate to a whopping 15 million Americans every other year.[2] And social anxiety isn't just endemic to America. It is global and inclusive; it transcends culture, social status, age, and religion. But there's also some good news there. With how common social anxiety is, there is hope for improvement. This book focuses on social anxiety in teens because that's the most affected group. This book is geared towards helping teens overcome social anxiety and live their lives to the fullest.

CHAPTER 2
# THE SYMPTOMS, ROOT CAUSES, AND IDENTIFYING FACTORS

Studies show that teenage anxiety has increased tremendously in the last few years. The journal of *Social Psychiatry and Psychiatric Epidemiology* reports that the number of teenagers who were positively screened for social anxiety increased from 34.1% to 44% between 2012 and 2018.[1] These reports highlight the steady increase in the prevalence of social anxiety among teenagers. Moreover, these numbers have been increasing unwaveringly in the last 20 years. The National Institute of Mental Health (NIMH) reports that social anxiety impacts a staggering 32.3% of teens aged 17-18, 32.1% of teens aged 15-16, and another 31.4% of teens aged 13-14.[2]

Experts believe that the real numbers could be much higher. As teens would rather not admit that they have social anxiety or seek help. Still, these alarming statistics indicate that teenage anxiety is a real and significant public health problem. The report also highlights the higher risks associated with certain age groups compared to others. For example, the same study, published by *Social Psychiatry and Psychiatric Epidemiology*, shows that females were at a higher risk of experiencing social anxiety.[1]

So, the big question is, what are the symptoms, root and risk causes, and identifying factors of social anxiety in teens? Why is social anxiety on the rise? What are some of the most common identifying factors? We've discussed some causes in chapter 1, but this chapter deeply delves into the real issues causing and aggravating social anxiety in teens. Research and experts in child development have provided some amazing insights on these issues.

## SYMPTOMS OF SOCIAL ANXIETY DISORDER

Social anxiety is broad and could manifest differently in different people, just like in the examples described in chapter 1. They could be acute or mild in different people and different scenarios. This means that your symptoms may not be the same as your friends who also struggle with social phobia. The intense fear and avoidance associated with social anxiety may be

## THE SYMPTOMS, ROOT CAUSES, AND IDENTIFYING FACTORS

limited to public speaking and starting or keeping up with small talk in certain individuals. At the same time, other people may be terrified of social settings, no questions asked. Understand that feeling shy or uncomfortable in social situations doesn't automatically mean someone has a social phobia. Comfort levels vary in all of us depending on personality types and life experiences. Some people are naturally outgoing and confident, while others are naturally laid back and reserved. Still, studies highlight some common ways social anxiety affects people.

**Physical symptoms**

The following symptoms often accompany social anxiety:

- Sweating.
- Blushing.
- Increased heart rate.
- Nausea.
- An upset stomach and diarrhea.
- Trouble breathing/shortness of breath.
- Lightheadedness.
- Dizziness.
- Choking or tightness around the chest.

- Muscle tension.
- "Going blank."
- Panic attacks in extreme situations.
- Difficulty concentrating.
- Fear of certain places and objects.
- Sleep problems.

These symptoms may come right before a feared event. Other times, you may spend weeks with these symptoms as you worry and await upcoming events. After the event, you spend endless hours nitpicking your performance and analyzing mistakes.

**Emotional symptoms**

You may constantly have:

- Extreme fear and avoidance of social situations or any setting where you may be judged negatively.
- Intense worry about humiliating, embarrassing, or degrading yourself.
- Crippling fear of interacting with strangers or talking to them.
- Constant worry that others will notice you.

## THE SYMPTOMS, ROOT CAUSES, AND IDENTIFYING FACTORS

- Feeling anxious and uncomfortable around others.
- Intense fear of physical symptoms that may give away your social anxiety, such as sweaty hands, blushing, shaky voice, and trembling.
- Extreme embarrassment which can lead to avoidance of social interactions or speaking with people.
- Intense fear of situations that make you the center of attention, such as public speaking or walking into a room full of people.
- Acute anxiety while awaiting a feared event, particularly social events.
- Crippling fear in social settings.
- Over-analysis of past performances and interactions.
- Picking apart perceived flaws and mistakes after social interactions.
- Always anticipating the worst consequences and interactions from social interactions.
- Fear of talking to authoritative figures.

**You may also have trouble with the following:**

- Making eye contact.
- Dating and going on dates.
- Talking to and interacting with strangers.
- Initiating conversations.
- Attending parties or other social gatherings.
- Going to school or work (if you work), you may create excuses not to go.
- Having trouble walking into rooms full of people.
- Going to the store either to buy or return items.
- Eating around others.
- Using public washrooms.

These symptoms are not always constant. They may shift occasionally and over time flare up when you are highly stressed.

## RISK FACTORS AND ROOT CAUSES THAT CONTRIBUTE TO SOCIAL ANXIETY DISORDER IN TEENS

Social anxiety disorder is extremely complex, and so are the factors contributing to it. For this reason, experts admit that it is quite challenging to identify the specific factors that lead to it. Sometimes what's thought to be a cause could be a contributing factor, and another believed to be a contributing factor could be the cause itself. Social phobia is also believed to result from a combination of influencing factors, which can be classified into three categories: life experiences, biological, and environmental factors.

## LIFE EXPERIENCES

Many teens develop social anxiety due to trauma caused by certain events. These incidents could be life-changing and can affect them to a great degree. Some of them include the following:

**Bullying**

Unfortunately, the world is full of mean people who'll stop at nothing to put others down. And teens are particularly prone to bullying, not just from their peers in school but also from the people they interact with online. Many teenagers agree that their social anxiety was either caused or aggravated by bullying, particularly after they were publicly shamed or humiliated.[6] For example, many teens bullied at school try their best to avoid school. After all, many of them feel threatened, isolated, lonely, and unsafe at school. They don't see the world and school, in general, as safe places for them. Many struggle with low self-esteem, low self-worth, self-hatred, helplessness, and hopelessness and often perform poorly in school. They may show physical symptoms of anxiety like fear and have a deep-seated desire to help other bullying victims but wouldn't know how to help them, being victims themselves. For this reason, they may harbor guilt for not helping others or acting on their behalf.

The pain and trauma associated with bullying stay with victims for a while, long after the bully finds another victim. It could be cyberbullying, name-calling, threats, or other types of bullying, but after prolonged exposure, the victim is bound to develop adverse reactions. Sadly, most children who are being bullied don't tell anyone. Older boys are even less likely to report bullying.[3] It's, therefore, important for parents to pay attention to any behavioral or emotional changes in their kids so that they can pick up on specific changes.

How do you tell if your socially anxious child is being bullied?

- They may have trouble sleeping.

## THE SYMPTOMS, ROOT CAUSES, AND IDENTIFYING FACTORS

- They are in a state of sadness.
- Have a sudden change in their desire to attend school.
- Experience constant physical ailments.
- Appear to have lost and damaged belongings.

But why do bullies target those with social anxiety? There are many reasons why socially anxious kids are an easier target for bullies. As it is, bullies love to pick on kids who:

- Have fewer friends.
- Those who are less assertive and confident.
- Kids who appear vulnerable or lacking in self-esteem.
- Have problems creating and maintaining friendships.
- Those with poor social skills.

Kids with low self-esteem are unlikely to stand up for themselves, and those with few friends are unlikely to defend themselves or have someone else do it on their behalf.

Experts have, in recent years, used rodents such as

mice and rats to investigate the long-term effects of bullying. Why rodents, you may ask? Well, studies show that rodents have similar stress responses to humans, so this research is critical. In one study, several mice were kept close to a mouse bully for several days, and changes in their brains were examined. The researchers learned that the hormone known as vasopressin was activated in the stressed mice, making their brains highly sensitive to social stimuli. After exposure to the stress, the bullied mice kept to themselves, avoiding all mice around them, even the friendly ones who hadn't bullied them. This could be a confirmation that humans react the same to bullying. Chronic bullying can increase an individual's stress hormone levels and significantly reduce social behavior.[3]

Researchers also found that:

- The symptoms of social anxiety disorder were increased in bullied adolescents.
- Socially anxious teen boys are more likely to be bullied.
- It's extremely hard for children with social anxiety to report bullying.

## Speech problems and other physical disabilities that draw attention

Teens with speech problems are often sensitive and conscious about themselves and how they speak. Because speech problems affect their confidence, they may worry about how people perceive them, especially when speaking. For this reason, many would rather avoid social situations.

Other disabilities, such as facial disfigurements, draw more attention to an individual, which could make a teen or any other person extremely self-conscious. It could have a negative impact on how a teen interacts with people around them, especially strangers.

I've also mentioned that sometimes what causes social anxiety overlaps with aggravating factors. Sometimes, speech problems can lead to social anxiety or cause social anxiety. For example, social anxiety can also lead to slurred speech and other problems resembling slurred speech.

The following are potential links between anxiety and speech problems and slurred speech:

*Overactive thoughts*: Anxiety can make it hard for someone to focus, which may lead to slurred speech. Stress can also interfere with mental clarity and recall. This extreme social anxiety may lead you to be "so far in your head" that getting your words out becomes problematic. Simply put, anxiety works your head and brain too hard, and when this happens, your brain loses focus on some of the most important things it should be doing— like speaking.

***Muscle tension*:** Anxiety has been linked to severe muscle tension, making it harder for someone to move their mouth muscles. This is usually the leading cause of slurred speech in certain conditions.

***Over-awareness*:** An interesting thing about social anxiety is that it makes you highly self-aware of behaviors others consider normal and automatic. This often happens in other areas of your life as well. For example, social anxiety may interfere with your speech or worsen it, but it can also make it harder for someone to walk because they are extremely aware of their leg movements. While speech is an automatic movement, during moments of extreme anxiety, you, and not your subconscious mind, may end up controlling your mouth movements, making them much harder to do.

*Anxiety medications*: Some speech issues are caused or worsened by anxiety symptoms. Most anxiety medications are also muscle relaxants and may interfere with the movement of face and mouth muscles. Always discuss your options for treatment and medication with a licensed healthcare provider. Take the medication as prescribed by a pharmacist or as instructed by your doctor.

**Personality and temperament**

This is often something you can't control. Some people are naturally shy, timid, withdrawn, and quiet. They are unwilling to explore the world and interact with the people around them. Such teens are at an increased risk of developing a social anxiety disorder.

**Abuse**

Research shows that all forms of physical, emotional, and sexual abuse could negatively impact a teen's social life. It's even worse when the issues are not addressed, and proper counseling isn't provided.

In such situations, abuse could lead to chronic social phobias.[4]

**Adolescence stage**

Our bodies go through significant changes during the adolescent stage. Many teens have a tough time adjusting to the mental and emotional changes experienced during this time. They struggle with their new perceptions and role in the home and general academic and social environments. All these issues combined give teenagers a unique set of challenges to overcome. Many will try to avoid social situations, fearing that people will notice the changes in their bodies and judge them.

**Current stresses and new social demands**

Studies show that "current stresses" could significantly impact a teen's level of social phobia. For example, moving away from a familiar location and cutting off ties with long-term friends and family could affect how a teen interacts with others. They have to start over, create new friendships, build new relationships, and meet new people. This all may take work, especially when they've had the same group of friends for a long time. They are already self-conscious, so going out and meeting new people can be more challenging.

**Trauma**

Divorce, separation, domestic violence, frequent shifts, and transfers in a child's developmental years could affect their ability to interact with others in their adolescent and adult years. Trauma may also result from discrimination (sex, social class, and religion), as well as addictions and withdrawal from drugs, biases, prejudices, and previous experiences with mental illness.

Research has shown that the development and gravity of social anxiety are higher in people who've experienced traumas and chronic stress. Other common traumatic events predictive of social anxiety include physical, sexual, and emotional abuse, family wrangles such as separation and custody battles; abandonment and neglect; loss of loved ones (family members or pets), stress during pregnancy or infancy, and postnatal depression.[5]

There is a direct link between traumatic experiences in childhood years and severe social anxiety in adolescent and adult years. This often leads to low self-esteem and a low sense of self-worth in people with social anxiety.

**Medical conditions**

Certain thyroid, heart, and lung conditions have been linked to social anxiety disorders. They can either cause or aggravate existing symptoms.[6]

## BIOLOGICAL FACTORS

Social anxiety disorder, like many other mental health disorders, can result from complex biological factors you may not have control over. Consider the examples discussed below.

**Family history**

Anxiety disorders can be inherited because they tend to run in the family. If a close relative, for example, a parent or sibling, suffers from social anxiety, then there's a 2-3% increased chance that those close to them will develop it. This isn't to say that they will develop it, only that the chances are increased, unlike in families with no history of a mental health disorder. Still, experts don't have a definitive answer as to how this happens and how much family history impacts or aggravates mental health.[7]

**Genetics**

While no particular gene has been linked directly to social anxiety disorder so far, experts believe that there is a high chance genetics do play a factor. In a study done to analyze the impact of genetics and its link to social anxiety disorder, experts gathered information on twins, and the results showed high levels of discordance. When one twin showed signs and symptoms of social phobia, the other twin also showed an increased likelihood of developing social phobia. This indicates that there could be a link between genes passed down from parents to children as it relates to social anxiety disorder.[8]

**Neurological factors and brain structure**

Studies show that sometimes, the amygdala, a portion of the brain that deals with anxiety, is hyperactive with people who have a social anxiety disorder. The amygdala also plays a significant role in the fight and flight response. Because it is hyperactive in these individuals, it could cause an exaggerated fear response, resulting in increased anxiety in certain situations.[9]

People with an overactive amygdala also show deficit production in feel-good hormones such as dopamine and serotonin.

## ENVIRONMENTAL FACTORS

Social anxiety doesn't always result from biological factors and life experiences; it is sometimes learned, particularly in the home setting. The home environment is the first setup a child is exposed to, and they learn and absorb things from it. If parents are overprotective or create anxious behavior in social situations, a child may pick up on it and internalize it. They could then replicate the same social behaviors they learned from their primary caregivers.

Other people also show signs of social anxiety after a negative or embarrassing social interaction.

## WHAT ROLES DO SOCIAL MEDIA AND OTHER TECHNOLOGICAL STRESSES PLAY?

**Technological stresses**

## THE SYMPTOMS, ROOT CAUSES, AND IDENTIFYING FACTORS

We live in a complex world where more than half our lives are online. We must update our social media friends on where we are, who we are with, what we are doing, and what we have. We must keep up with them too, and figure out everything they do with their lives. A teenager's life is already hard as it is. Add the pressure of modern technology, and you have a ticking time bomb. There's always a feeling that there is more you need to do to fit in, be beautiful enough, or be considered cool enough.

Moreover, you don't need any verbal skills to interact with people online. This means that there are fewer real-life social interactions which ultimately reduces the opportunities to practice and polish social skills. This could result in extreme anxiety, particularly when one finds themselves in a social situation where one must interact with others.

**Social media**

As adults struggle to make sense of the rising cases of social anxiety in teens, they cannot help but notice a common link that runs through this epidemic—something that previous generations didn't have to deal with. Stuck in every teen's hand is a smartphone, sending in endless notifications of social media updates and other things they should be checking. Many parents are sick of this and would rather grab the phone and lock it somewhere they can't find it. But that isn't practical. Unless they want to come across as controlling and overprotective, which could also lead to social anxiety. It's no surprise, therefore, that developmental experts believe that increased screen time and endless social media use have led to an uptick in social anxiety in teens.

According to a 2015 Pew Study, social media comes with many stressors that can trigger social anxiety.[10] You see people posting about parties and events you weren't invited to. This makes you feel left out like you don't fit in with the cool kids. You often feel pressure to post parts of your life that show you in a positive and attractive light. Anything less is unacceptable. This means you must try to find positive aspects of your life to post or fake them. There is constant pressure to get enough likes, comments, and shares because it reflects how attractive, likable, and cool you are. What's more, you hate it when someone posts something about you because it's beyond your control.

Recent studies show a significant increase in suicidal thoughts and social anxiety among teens, particularly those who spend many hours glued to

## THE SYMPTOMS, ROOT CAUSES, AND IDENTIFYING FACTORS

their screens.[11] Still, some pressures associated with teen anxiety are consistent with normal concerns associated with self-expression and social standing around that developmental age. Indeed, social media has exacerbated social anxiety. Still, it's also crucial for parents to know where their child's particular stressors lie and how they can tailor solutions to their children's anxieties.

Studies show a direct and significant rise in loneliness, dependence, worry, anxiety, and sleeplessness in teens that directly coincides with the release of the first iPhone over a decade ago. The study showed that up to 48% of teens who spent at least five hours every other day on an electronic device reported at least one suicide risk factor. This is in contrast to the 33% of teens who spend less than two hours on a given electronic device.[12] And we are all familiar with the endless anecdotes of teens who are constantly reduced to tears from the endless comparison social media brings.

Through the number of followers, likes, comments, and mentions one has, teenagers, have actual data on how many people like or even dislike them and how they look. An overwhelming amount of social media pressure comes from how many people liked, shared, or disliked their content. That's because

33

this data gives a rough idea about what others think of them. This complicates the problem further because kids are extremely focused on how they look during their teenage years. And none of these teens are getting a break from technology. Gone are the days when teens had a break from social pressure. They could go back home, be alone and digest everything that happened at school. Kids don't have that kind of luxury these days. When they get home, they grab their phones and continue the cycle that started in school.

It's true that so many things teenagers struggle with today, in the wake of technological advancements and social media, are challenges that have been around for decades. Still, they've certainly been aggravated because they are now taking place in a different space. These spaces amplify and shift the size, quantity, and quality of these developmental challenges. The desire to fit in, the importance of peer friendships and associations, the need to figure out which version of yourself you like best, and how to express that identity to others aren't new.

Other challenges include feeling replaceable. You are under constant pressure to like your friends' pictures promptly, because if you don't, someone else will, and they'll come across as a better friend, and you may end up in the background. Another issue associated with social media is Fear of Missing Out or FoMo. If you aren't all caught up with the latest social media posts, you feel uncool, more like you'll be left out of real-life conversations at school tomorrow. Then, there is the real attachment to devices, feeling like you'll look like a bad friend if you miss a message from a friend who needs you.

For this reason, you are never away from your phone. Simply put, teens have their sense of self-worth grounded in social media. But social media is like a drug; you can never have enough. You always need to do more to please people, and when they aren't as pleased as you'd like them to be, you feel unworthy, like you aren't good enough.

## SOCIAL PRESSURE TO LOOK GOOD AND SUCCEED ACADEMICALLY

Our society is becoming increasingly modernized by the day. With that comes an overwhelming pressure to succeed academically, professionally, and in all areas of our lives. The cost of higher education is rising, and youth face a fierce job market even when they've graduated. For this reason, teens are constantly bombarded by anxiety-causing messages of success and achievements. They constantly feel pressure to earn a given GPA, participate in certain extracurricular activities and excel at them, or score specific grades to qualify for particular scholarships. The pressure to excel in sports means teenagers must spend endless hours training and on the road making their way to compete in different competitions.

With so much pressure to succeed, teens are more driven and motivated to succeed, at the sacrifice of their emotional well-being. There's a lot of pressure to get it right. You must balance all the demands of transitioning from childhood to independent adulthood and be as successful as possible. This is extremely overwhelming for a developing brain. And this is particularly hard for teens who feel like their performance is less than ideal. They are scared others will judge them, their parents will scold them, and they'll probably never make it to good colleges or universities.

A new study also highlights the stress associated with the desire to look good. In the study, the author writes that approximately 64% of parents admitted that their teenagers are extremely self-conscious about their bodies. There's at least one aspect of their appearance that they are worried about. Maybe it's their weight, breast size, skin, height, hair, or how clothes fit them. The study showed that the level of self-consciousness in teens was so bad that more than 27% of the study participants reported a negative impact on their self-confidence. Up to 20% of teens said they didn't want to participate in social activities because of how they felt about their bodies. Some even refused to appear in photos, while others tried to hide their appearance using clothing. Moreover, close to 10% of the study's teens were involved in restrictive eating.[13]

Even worse, many parents said their teenagers had been bullied by other children, family members, healthcare providers, strangers, and teachers, because of their appearance. These teenagers were also aware they were being treated differently because of their appearance, which worsened their social anxiety. We already know that a negative self-image aggravates anxiety, leads to low self-esteem, low self-confidence, and ultimately, low emotional and mental health.

Body dissatisfaction is strongly linked to social anxiety and other risk-taking behavior. Another study on teens in the UK highlighted and revealed some mind-blowing findings. An estimated 36% of teens in the survey said they are more than willing to do whatever it takes to look good to fit in with others. Up to 57% percent said they had tried diets, while another

10% admitted that they had thought about doing surgeries to change certain things and, again, fit in. The boys in the study said they were willing to take steroids to achieve their goals.[14]

Studies show that teenagers with poor body image often avoid healthy behaviors. Some admit they were less likely to engage in sports or exercise because they were too self-conscious or scared that someone was watching. Up to 24% of boys and 36% of girls in the study admitted to avoiding social activities like physical education because of their appearance. The poor self-image was also directly linked to alcohol and drug use, with teenagers who showed greater body appreciation avoiding those things. In contrast, those with a poor self-image were reportedly more willing to indulge. The pressure to be thin and other body dissatisfaction issues are strongly linked to extreme social anxiety symptoms, particularly in teens who don't match society's expectation of an "ideal body." Symptoms of social anxiety and other mental health illnesses were particularly pronounced in obese and overweight teenagers, according to the same study.[14]

The study also revealed that many teenagers internalized the messages of an ideal body image they saw on social media and those perpetrated by the media.

Such teens felt the need to live up to certain body images and appearances and felt shame and discomfort when they didn't meet those standards. Up to 37% of teens said they felt angry about their bodies, and another 31% said they were ashamed of their appearance.[14]

The pressure was worse in girls, as these insecurities are often more pronounced in women. Girls feel the need to stay thin but maintain their curves, while teenage boys admit that they would be more satisfied if they were tall and muscular. Because some didn't meet these standards, they felt bad about themselves, translating to many hours spent on social media doing appearance-related comparisons and peer competition. These same teenagers who had issues with body image were also victims of appearance-based cyberbullying, which worsened an already fragile self-image. Teenagers who had been cyberbullied were twice as likely to struggle with social anxiety, with many describing themselves as "too fat." In fact, up to 59% of teens who had been cyberbullied about their appearance struggled with social anxiety in one way or another, and 29% were depressed.[14]

## PEER PRESSURE AND THE NEED FOR ACCEPTANCE

Everyone wants to fit in and be accepted and loved for who they are. This is particularly crucial for teenagers, who are still trying to figure out their identity and see how it fits with friends and society. Teenagers feel the impact of peer pressure more intensely and to varying degrees. As it is, our peers influence us significantly. We often look to them for guidance, reassurance, and a sense of belonging. This means that peer pressure is a persuasive force that affects teens' mental health. While peer pressure is synonymous with teenage years, studies show that humans love to fit in from a young age. Peer pressure could be positive when it is about academic achievement, co-curricular activities, doing sports together, and sticking to constructive behavior. But peer pressure can also be negative, where a teen feels the need to engage in reckless sexual activity, try out drugs and alcohol, or participate in risky behavior just to fit in.[15]

The impact of such negative behavior is low self-confidence and self-worth and distancing from loved ones. Studies show a direct link between social anxiety, depression, and peer pressure among teens. At its worst, depression could lead to self-harm, suicidal thoughts, and other risky behavior. According to an article published by EducationWeek, studies also show that peer pressure is a powerful predictor of chronic sleep issues, increased stress levels, and extreme social anxiety symptoms. And social media has made this harder because now, a teen's peer group has constant access to them outside regular school hours. Teenagers look at peer groups as a way to build friendships and social support. The fear of isolation and ridicule is huge for them. Studies show that teenagers are wired for peer approval.[16]

## PARENTING STYLE AND PARENTAL DISAPPROVAL

Studies show a strong link between parenting style and teen social anxiety disorder. This is particularly relevant when the parents are overprotective, controlling, restrictive and anxious. An overprotective parent stands in the way of their child's ability to have healthy social interactions with their peers or take risks that challenge and grow them. Ultimately, the sheltered child grows up lacking opportunities to learn essential skills that would sharpen their coping skills in certain situations.[17]

When parents are quick to criticize, slow in showing affection, controlling, and extremely worried about other people's opinions, then the child suffers. Their parent's actions and words often shape a child's self-image and perception of the world. For this reason, children who grow up in such home environments tend to be fearful, less trustworthy, and more self-conscious. In most cases, parents don't notice how much their actions affect their children, but their disapproval sets them up for a difficult social life later. Even worse, parents who are dismissive or who often invalidate their children's feelings and concerns about social anxiety may contribute significantly to the condition worsening.

The following example demonstrates how parenting experiences can lead to social anxiety. As she was growing up, Amy's parents forbade her from playing sports because they feared she would be injured. Because these were her parents and Amy was too young to know any better, she accepted their arguments as reasonable. To protect herself from all the dangers they described, Amy completely avoided all forms of social interactions and eventually developed social anxiety.

Other parents and primary caregivers can instill social anxiety in their kids by negatively labeling social opportunities as "dangerous" rather than challenging. If they don't clarify the benefits of social

## THE SYMPTOMS, ROOT CAUSES, AND IDENTIFYING FACTORS

interactions to those kids, the children may only interpret them as sources of social anxiety. Children can also learn to interpret ambiguous behavior as anxiety-provoking situations. A random glance or stare in their direction could lead to rumination about what that means for them.

Some children are also born with what experts call behaviorally inhibited temperaments. Such children often experience distress and withdraw from unfamiliar environments, people, or situations. This avoidance behavior can start as early as infancy. Sometimes, children exhibit anxiety symptoms, such as crying, hiding from strangers, irritability, and moving around. Children may also show signs of unhealthy clingy behavior around their parents, especially in the presence of strangers. Some children may also show indifference and an extremely limited range of emotions in the presence of caregivers and strangers. Studies show that such children are more likely to develop social anxiety as teenagers and adults.[18]

Other children overreact to things, a scenario often described as hypersensitivity. Speed of reactivity is also a well-known contributing factor to anxiety. It describes the rate at which different people react to things. People who react fast to situations are more likely to develop anxiety and may quickly show signs of anxiety, such as increased heart rate and faster breathing rate. Studies also show that teens with a family history of anxiety disorder are more likely to show signs of behavioral inhibitions.[18]

A study published by The Journal of Child and Family Studies indicates that these temperaments can lead to the development of or aggravate social anxiety and social anxiety disorder.[19]

Another issue similar to this is some children's insecure attachment style. Two distinct attachment styles are associated with social anxiety disorder.

**1.** *Anxious-Ambivalent Insecure Attachment:* This attachment style describes children who are overly anxious about exploration or interaction with strangers, even when their primary caregivers are around.

**2.** *Anxious-Avoidant Insecure Attachment:* This would describe children who aren't interested in exploring their surroundings whether or not the primary caregiver is around. Most of them are more or less indifferent, showing little emotional range toward strangers and the primary caregiver—usually the mother.

According to a study from Kent State University, children with these attachment styles are more likely to develop social anxiety down the line.[20] From a young age, these children have learned and perfected the art of withdrawing from stressful and unfamiliar situations and people. The avoidance reinforces anxious behavior later in life, which is often viewed as some protective response.

Understand also that attachment style and temperament are classified as both genetic and environmental contributors to social anxiety. This is why I created a separate section for the two because they are neither exclusively genetic nor environmental.

## IDENTIFYING FACTORS

Identifying factors of social anxiety differ in teenagers based on their personalities, temperaments, and how much they can recognize and are willing to share. Some people have mild, while others have moderate or extreme forms of social anxiety. Other people only experience symptoms of social anxiety in a single type of situation, such as eating around others or performing in front of strangers. In contrast, others experience different types of social anxiety-related symptoms in multiple settings.

In general, social anxiety can manifest in three different ways:

**1. *Mild social anxiety:*** A child with mild social anxiety will experience its physical and psychological symptoms but still be able to participate and endure social interactions. They may also only feel uncomfortable in certain situations.

**2. *Moderate social anxiety:*** In this case, a child with social anxiety will experience the physical and psychological symptoms of social anxiety in specific settings and still participate in them but avoid other social settings altogether.

**3. *Extreme social anxiety:*** People with extreme social anxiety struggle with intense physical and psychological symptoms of social anxiety, such as panic attacks in social settings. For this reason, most of them avoid social situations altogether. When someone has extreme social anxiety, they'll have most of the symptoms mentioned at the beginning

## THE SYMPTOMS, ROOT CAUSES, AND IDENTIFYING FACTORS

of the chapter in most, if not all, social settings.

It is common for teenagers with social anxiety to have anticipatory anxiety when faced with certain social situations. Sometimes, they also experience symptoms ranging from mild to extreme social anxiety.

A healthcare worker, such as a therapist, psychiatrist, or doctor, uses the criteria for social anxiety highlighted in the fifth edition of the Diagnostic and Statistical Manual of Mental Disorders (DSM-5) to identify social anxiety. The American Psychiatric Association published this manual.[21] To be classified as social anxiety, a person's symptoms should include the following:

- Continuous, intense fear and anxiety in social situations because they are extremely worried and scared of being judged negatively or humiliated by people around them.
- Avoiding social situations that may make them anxious, or they may put up with them but still experience extreme fear and anxiety.

- Continuous, intense anxiety that is disproportionate to the threat of the social situation.
- Experiencing extreme anxiety, stress, and distress that interferes with their daily life.
- Extreme fear and anxiety in social situations that aren't exactly explainable as a medical condition or caused by substance abuse.

The healthcare provider determines whether you fit the social anxiety criteria by asking about your history and symptoms. They may also do a physical exam and ask about medications you've taken in the past or if you have certain medical conditions that may have led to the anxiety. To be diagnosed with social anxiety, a person must have had these symptoms for at least six months before the diagnosis.[22]

# CHAPTER 3
# THE EFFECTS OF SOCIAL ANXIETY

I struggled with social anxiety for the better part of my teenage years. When I was a teen walking to a new school, I quickly realized that the bus had dropped me off 40 minutes before my first class started. I was trying to think about what I could do with that time. I wanted to be by myself, sitting in a corner—be alone. But I feared people would negatively judge me, wondering who's that loser with no friends. So, I devised a plan: I'd walk the hallways over and over again for 40 minutes until my class started instead of sitting alone in a class where everyone would look at me. And I thought to myself, this would be great, and no one will ever know what I was doing. Until one day, someone did.

I got on the bus to head home from school, and somebody called me out in front of everybody and said,

## SOCIAL ANXIETY AS A TEEN

*"Why do you walk the halls in circles every morning?"* I felt my heart suddenly drop down to my stomach. I was so ashamed, humiliated, and embarrassed. I knew the next day at school that I could not walk the hallways again. From that day forward, I'd go to school, go to the bathroom, lock myself in, and cry. I'd have these thoughts like, "*Why can't you talk to people?" "Why can't you make friends?" "Why aren't you normal?* I don't want you to go through the same experiences I did in high school. In this section, I'll talk about the major effects of social anxiety, because the first step towards overcoming it is understanding how it affects you.

### NEGATIVE IMPACT ON CONFIDENCE

Feeling incompetent, awkward, uncomfortable, or generally bad about ourselves is normal. Even people we think are the most confident sometimes suffer from these feelings of inadequacy. But if these feelings become intense and chronic, you'll suffer from low self-confidence.

You may find yourself shying away from taking healthy risks or constantly telling yourself or others that you are not good enough, attractive enough, or smart enough. You may find yourself saying things like, "I am so stupid. Why can't I do anything right?" All these are signs of low self-esteem and lack of confidence in yourself. Unchecked social anxiety can break down your self-confidence and leave you feeling unworthy.

## DIFFICULTIES IN STUDIES

Social anxiety locks a teen's brain, making school life and social connections difficult. Going to school can be an issue if you doubt you'll succeed or when you want to avoid certain people. The Anxiety and Depression Association of America revealed that teens with low self-esteem and self-confidence are more likely to avoid school tasks.[1] Sometimes you feel you've not studied enough or don't know anything and can't put up with your colleagues.

You might also fear being around your teachers because their teaching styles don't match your personality. Strict teachers with rigid teaching styles might worsen your anxiety leading to your failure in your studies. You'll be afraid to ask them a question individually or during class. You might also look uninterested when you start skipping school-related activities like giving presentations, joining group work, or missing school functions. But the opposite is true. You are struggling with social phobia.

## MISSING OUT ON LIFE

Social anxiety blocks you from living your life to the fullest. Even worse, it leads you to avoid situations that people consider normal. You'll find it difficult to understand how people handle those situations. You might not even understand how someone can ask a beautiful girl for a date. The result? You miss out on developing a romantic relationship with another person, yet it's a normal stage of growing up. It gets even worse because your abnormal behavior starts to bother you. And here, your anxiety piles up even more.

Avoiding phone calls is another effect of social phobia. Anxiety is a feeling we can all relate to, but when you avoid a phone call, it probably means you're so scared of the evaluation judgment that may happen when you are on a phone call.

Social anxiety can make you feel lost in your fear and discomfort. Since you are so much into your worries, you might be unaware of people around you, even family. You might miss out on a family discussion that would be a chance to share problems you're experiencing personally or at school. As a result, more pressure and anxiety build up.

What's more, you'll have difficulties attending social gatherings and parties if you have a social phobia. And it is in these hangouts you learn new things and update yourself with what's happening in your circle. That way, you feel a sense of relevance in life and not a waste of space. So, if you have social anxiety, you'll avoid social interactions, leaving you with poor social skills, a lack of identity, and no sense of belonging.

You might be talented in dancing, soccer, acting, or any other field, but social anxiety cuts you off. You might fear that you will embarrass yourself or look dumb while performing in front of your peers or a large group of people. You lose an opportunity to showcase your craft and another to improve it.

## CONSTANT NEED AND PRESSURE TO FIT IN

When the Center for Adolescent Health asked teenagers what their major challenge in adolescence was, they didn't say meeting their parents' expectations or maintaining good grades. It was the issue of fitting in. Their worst fear was finding a social group they could be a part of.[2]

Of course, you don't want people to see you spending time alone in school. And indeed, you don't want to join groups that the rest of the school doesn't like. You know, the freaks, geeks, and nerds. At the same time, you come across a group you'd be glad to spend time with but don't know how to approach them. You dread rejection.

## THE CONSTANT NEED FOR VALIDATION FROM PEOPLE AROUND YOU

Social anxiety may make you unreasonably needy in the relationships you have. You need constant approval and validation even when you need to make important decisions. For example, when you finally get your dream job, a promotion, or that perfect date you've been waiting for, you have to ask those around you what they think or if it's a good decision you are making. It is normal to crave validation from your loved ones, but too much of it may affect your personality, emotions, and attachment style.

This phobia can give you trouble managing your current romantic relationship or pursuing a new one. You struggle communicating with your partner or opening up because you worry they might abandon you.

## UNSUCCESSFUL LIFE

While it's okay to experience anxiety at certain points in your life, from health concerns and relationship issues to family matters and unreasonable deadlines, if left untreated, social phobia can affect your relationship's life and career. It can hold you back from hitting your full potential in life.

Studies show that 40 million Americans struggle to succeed because of workplace anxiety.[3]

Here are three common ways social anxiety blocks you from leading a successful life:

1. *Loss of confidence:* Since social anxiety damages your self-esteem, you're already limited to a job that doesn't require much social interaction. Jobs like those of a data entry clerk or a security guard don't require you to do any presentation or talk to a group of people. That already decreases your income potential.

2. *Missed opportunities:* Most success stories come from taking advantage of opportunities, but when you have social anxiety, you may look at opportunities as challenges and avoid

them altogether. And because social anxiety entails fear, you tend to avoid such opportunities. Take a job interview, for example. It's not only nerve-racking but also panic-inducing. You're even worried about how you'll negotiate your paycheck. Even worse, if it happens you get the job, you're afraid of leadership positions because you don't speak too much and dread things like office politics. In the end, you let go of the chance.

3. *Loss of interest:* Often, chronic fear won't allow you to leave your comfort zone. For example, you're quiet at the workplace in a meeting—wanting nothing to do with anyone and having nothing to contribute. You just hope the day ends sooner because you are always uncomfortable around your colleagues. While your lack of interest in anything limits your exposure to opportunities, it also builds a barrier between you and colleagues who could have helped you further your career.

# CHAPTER 4
# CHALLENGE YOUR PERSONAL BEHAVIORS

A World Health Organization (WHO) survey cited that seven out of ten pre-teens and teens have experienced a mental disorder, and 80% have gone through social anxiety.[1] And we all know that teenage life is a troubled period for many. Understandably, as a teen, you have overwhelming decisions about lifestyle, career, friends, sex, and more. Making these decisions and planning what direction your life will take can be incredibly stressful and drive you to anxiety if you're not well-equipped to deal with the situations you face. To enjoy a crisis-free teenage life and come out as a responsible adult, you should possess skills like goal-setting, decision-making, and assertiveness. Even more, you must be able to control your life completely. You must first assess, review, and challenge your behaviors to achieve all these. By the end of the process, you'll see what areas of your life social anxiety affects.

Here's how you can handle the process:

## LIFE CHOICES FOR PHYSICAL HEALTH

**Working out**

Social anxiety can stand in the way of trying something new and putting yourself out there. But working out can help you beat your fears, relax, and make new friends. Trying new things will help you suppress your fears. Creating an exercise plan, like having a regular swimming schedule or joining a team, can help you overcome the fear of failing, social interactions, or embarrassment. It might take time, but the results are worth it.

Working out reduces stress and makes you feel good and relaxed by releasing a chemical called endorphins.[2] Cycling, running, and walking are excellent ways for individual workouts if you feel like you are not prepared or ready enough to exercise in groups, join group sports, or organized training.

Joining a dance league or a sports team lets you meet new people with similar interests. Team sports encourage bonding and communication because they require you to participate and contribute to your team. You'll find nothing to worry about or feel embarrassed about because you'll be participating in the same thing. Focusing on positive things—exercising, for example, removes your anxious mind from things that make you nervous. Your anxiety worsens because of your high concentration on anxiety-inducing issues. So, getting out of that anxious-engulfed world into a positive one reduces social stress.

**Eating healthy**

Some research suggests that transitioning to healthy eating habits and eating foods rich in nutrients can help ease anxiety symptoms in some people and serve as a helpful tool in managing anxiety. Eating healthy foods helps ease symptoms of anxiety. Some foods contribute to anxiety, while other substances affect the body and brain differently. For example, teens love snacks, but they contain high levels of unhealthy sugar and fats and are more likely to cause anxiety than foods rich in vitamins and minerals like vegetables, lean meat, fruits, proteins, and carbohydrates. Processed foods and sugar may lead to inflammation in your brain and body. This inflammation can contribute to depression, mood swings, and anxiety.[3]

When depressed or stressed, we often reach for processed foods for a quick fix. And when we are in a difficult period or very busy, we opt for unhealthy food options like coffee or fast food. Most of the time, this habit becomes a vicious cycle and does nothing positive for our health. Besides brain and body inflammation, we gain weight and feel sluggish, leading to lost confidence. All of these things combined may lead to social anxiety eventually.

But healthy foods improve our overall mental and physical health. In addition to eating healthy, taking water to keep your body hydrated, avoiding alcohol, and limiting caffeine, there are more considerations to help reduce anxiety. Complex carbohydrates, for example, metabolize slowly and help keep a balanced sugar level, giving you a calmer feeling. Foods rich in fiber, like whole grains, are healthier than those with simple, refined carbohydrates, mainly found in processed foods. Remember not to skip your meals either because when you do, your blood sugar may drop, giving you a jittery feeling and worsening underlying anxiety.

**Drugs and alcohol**

## CHALLENGE YOUR PERSONAL BEHAVIORS

Drugs and alcohol abuse in teenagers is a common problem. Despite how common this problem is, you should not take it lightly because it has severe social consequences now and in the future. Drug and alcohol abuse can bring or mask emotional issues such as depression or anxiety. These emotional problems often lead to severe mental health issues, which may result in suicide and self-harm. Research suggests that teenagers who use alcohol and drugs are at a higher risk of attempting or committing suicide than those who don't.[4]

The common misconception is that teens experimenting with alcohol and drugs are inherently 'bad kids,' and they get into this habit because they want to lash out and rebel. On a small percentage, this might be true. But it's not one-sided. The curiosity and peer pressure associated with teenage years may lead to drug and alcohol abuse, even in kids who would never attempt drug use. It's unfortunate, but sometimes teens feel like they have to engage in these activities to fit in and be accepted by their social circles.[5]

If you feel you are at a higher risk of alcohol or drug addiction, the following questions may highlight the seriousness of the problem.

- Have you ever taken alcohol or drugs in a way that endangers your life or those of others?
- Has the abuse of these substances caused conflict with others or family relationship problems?
- Have you failed to fulfill your school, home, or work responsibilities because of alcohol or drug abuse?
- When you don't take alcohol or drugs, do you feel the need to withdraw from everyone and everything?
- Have you built a tolerance to alcohol and drugs so that the more you take, the more the effect remains the same?
- Have you started using larger amounts of the substances?
- Have you tried to quit entirely but have been unsuccessful?

If you answered 'Yes' to at least four of these questions, you might be an addict.

Thankfully, the condition can be managed successfully, and research shows that the disorder is treatable.[6] There are rehab institutions all over the country equipped to help teenagers dealing with

CHALLENGE YOUR PERSONAL BEHAVIORS

alcohol or drug addiction. Whether you're addicted to one of them or both, seek medical attention immediately and start your journey to recovery.

## LIFESTYLE CHOICES FOR MENTAL HEALTH

**Time spent on social media**

The Pew Research Center indicates that up to 55% of teenagers spend their free time on social media, and up to 36% agree that they stay on social media way past bedtime trolling, texting, scrolling, sharing, shaming, bullying, you name it.[7] Of course, all these activities on Twitter, Snapchat, Instagram, or Facebook promote feelings of loneliness, poor body image, depression, and social anxiety. Social media has a 'culture of comparison' and can be damaging. If your number of likes, followers, or friends doesn't look like what your friends have, you might start questioning who you are and doubt your self-image. You'll look at yourself negatively, *"I'll never be like these people."* This mindset puts you at risk of isolation, depression, and social anxiety.

Spending more time online reduces your real, face-to-face interaction with your friends. This habit

## SOCIAL ANXIETY AS A TEEN

can lead to depression and social anxiety because you're not healthily engaging with the world. And the best way to fight social anxiety as a teen is to involve yourself in challenging situations. Be it speaking up in your class, participating in a debate, or joining several sports teams. But increasing your online presence will only aggravate your feelings of hopelessness, alienation, depression, and anxiety.

How can you tell you're spending too much time on social media?

1. You feel anxious and agitated when you cannot reach your social media handle.

Do you feel uncomfortable when you cannot log in to your social media account? This could mean your craving for social media is too strong.

*Solution:*
Keep your phone out of sight. If you're focusing on homework, leave your phone in the bedroom or another room. While at school, leave your phone at home.

2. Social media is your source of news.

Social media platforms are not places to turn to for news. They carry no news or only negative news and gossip, so you cannot rely on them.

*Solution:*

Get your daily news and updates from credential news sources such as authoritative websites and mainstream media houses.

3. You check your phone as soon as there is a notification.

Phone notifications give you a happy feeling. This happy feeling stems from a chemical in the brain called *dopamine*. According to research, *dopamine* is a crucial element in most addictions. The *dopamine* effect makes you feel like you're receiving a reward from your social networks, so whenever a notification pops in, you rush to check it out.

*Solution:*
Turn off your notifications.

**Talking poorly to yourself**

Poor self-talk affects your self-esteem. When you're down, you're likely to be hard on yourself and might judge and criticize yourself unfairly. Maybe you often find yourself saying, *"I completely messed up my exams; I'm a total loser and will never be successful in life!"* This talk is self-defeating poor talk and can discourage you from studying harder or putting in effort in other important areas of your life. Identifying this poor self-talk can be tricky because they are so automatic, and you might not even realize them. Nevertheless, when you feel upset, depressed, angry, or anxious, ask yourself the following questions: (*They'll help you look at your situation from a different perspective*).

- Are there facts and evidence to support my thoughts?
- Am I rushing to negative conclusions?
- Is my situation as bad as I see it?
- What's the worst that could happen?
- What can I learn from my situation?
- What else does my situation mean?

If your answers to these questions highlight a negative self-talk pattern, then try to change your thoughts and what you say to yourself. Replace poor self-talk with positive self-talk, and you'll feel better about yourself. For example, "*I'm in my jeans, and I look fat and ugly.*" Replace it with, "*My jeans look amazing today. Everyone complimented me on them.*"

**Low self-esteem**

If you often compare yourself to others, are quick to put off your achievements, and focus more on your shortcomings, then you're most likely suffering from low self-esteem.

Below I've compiled a list of questions common among teens with low self-esteem. Ask yourself these questions—that's the first step towards building your esteem and working on a better you.

1. Do you place little or no value on your thoughts?
2. Do you focus intensely on your shortcomings or weaknesses?
3. Are you quick to disregard your accomplishments or skills?
4. Do you compare yourself with others more often?
5. Do you reject or have a problem with positive corrections from others?

6. Are you very sensitive to criticism?
7. Do you take too long to make decisions because you're worried about what others will say?
8. Do you feel uncomfortable and anxious in social settings?
9. Are you the person you always looked forward to being?

If you answered "yes" to at least five of these questions, then you probably have low self-esteem and need more professional intervention for further support.

**Negative self-image**

Self-image is an inside job. Your internal attitudes, opinions, emotions, and thoughts shape what you think about yourself. And most of us have done this—talk and look at ourselves negatively. Most, if not all, of our negative self-image comes from our traumatic experiences with our friends, siblings, parents, or teachers. For example, let's say you posted a nice picture online, but your classmates decided to bully you for it. This could lead to a negative self-image of yourself. As a result of such experiences,

## CHALLENGE YOUR PERSONAL BEHAVIORS

you may build negative beliefs about your behavior and appearance. Although you cannot change your past, you can do a lot to adjust your expectations and thoughts on yourself and improve your perception of your self-image.

You probably have a negative image of yourself if you:

- Have trouble establishing relationships.
- Have fear of being the center of attention.
- Often downplay your success.
- Have difficulty making decisions, even small ones.
- Frequently compare yourself to your friends.

Try doing this instead:

- Say 'yes' to things you'd typically say 'no' to because you feel insecure when you say 'yes.'
- Ask a family member to help you pinpoint your positive personality qualities.
- Please keep track of good things happening in your life in the last two weeks and how they have made you feel.

- Please take note of negative thoughts about yourself and ask yourself whether they are worth your attention.
- Write down the benefits of improved self-confidence. Write what would change if you believed in yourself.

## LIFESTYLE CHOICES FOR EMOTIONAL HEALTH

**Fluctuating emotions**

Seemingly small events such as a drop in grades may result in a swing in emotions—some of which may be dramatic expressions. This is normal because you're reacting to a specific event. It's okay if the fluctuating emotions last for a day or two. But if it turns out that you're chronically sad and anxious, then that is beyond what is normal.

So, how do you tell when you're experiencing normal fluctuating emotions, when it has gone overboard, and you need treatment?

- If your emotional reactions overwhelm you so much that you have a problem functioning in many other parts of your

## CHALLENGE YOUR PERSONAL BEHAVIORS

life, say friendships, school, home, or work, such a situation needs evaluation.
- Fluctuating moods happening constantly for over two weeks; this is beyond the normal range.
- When disruptive feelings and thoughts prevent you from engaging in your day-to-day activities.
- Being unable to get out of bed because you're emotionally unstable.

**Constant mood swings**

Anxiety symptoms may bring a lot of emotional distress leading to mood swings. These mood fluctuations bring stress, nervousness, and fear.

Have you been experiencing the following fluctuation of emotions for more than two weeks non-stop?

- Extreme low moods.
- Feelings of up and downs.
- You feel a certain way, but you cannot explain why.

Also, ask yourself these two questions:

1. Have I been stuck in my mood recently?
2. Have my experiences in life become very difficult to deal with?

Take the following steps to ease your situation:

- Get socially engaged, with family and friends, for example.
- Adjust your diet. Find alternatives to junk foods.
- Create time for enough sleep.
- Get regular exercise. Even taking a daily walk will be helpful.

**Showing aggression or violent behavior toward others**

Excessive violence and aggression develop from disturbed emotional regulation, like abnormally low or high anxiety levels. Although a certain amount of aggression is typical and expected among teens, using insults, aggression, and violence toward others is unacceptable.

Here are a few tips to help deal with this situation:

***Behavioral contracts:*** as a parent, list the

behaviors you'd expect from your teenager and the reward they'll get from them.

***Relaxation techniques***: learn techniques such as deep breathing and practice them when you feel emotionally overwhelmed.

***Family counseling***: as a parent, involve a trained therapist in a regular family counseling session if you choose to.

**Arguing with those around you**

Often, social anxiety makes you feel incompetent and unable to handle a threat or a stressful environment. When this happens, anxiety turns into arguments, frustration, and anger. The problem with arguing is that it doesn't work because tension starts to build, you get personal, and you go back and forth without getting anywhere.

Here are four strategies to help you step back from arguments:

1. Take time to think and allow yourself to calm down. You also buy time for the other person to calm down.

*"Let me think about it."*

2. Acknowledging the other person's point of view. This will probably make them soften their position.

*"You might be right."*

For example, if someone says, *"You didn't handle that task well,"* and you disagree, you may respond with, *"You might be right."* This will help you avoid unnecessary arguments.

3. Listen.

*"I understand."*

These words may seem simple, but they change an argument's direction and eventually stop it because you've chosen to just listen.

4. Take responsibility.

*"I'm sorry for what I said. That's not what I meant."*

It shows a sense of responsibility and prevents things from getting worse.

## How you communicate with others

When feeling anxious, you may limit communication or even avoid it altogether. You might speak very softly or avoid eye contact. But you don't have to do this. Remember, communication is the foundation of being human. Without communication, it would be impossible to survive. It is, therefore, important to improve your communication skills as a teenager in high school, college, or the workplace. Better communication skills prepare you to succeed in the future.

Here's four ways how you can improve these skills:

1. Think before you talk.

Pause to arrange your words while paying close attention to how you say them and what to say.

2. Maintain a smile and a positive attitude.

You'll automatically receive a positive response when you show a positive attitude and a smile.

3. Review your messages before you send them.

Ask yourself how you'd feel if someone sent this message to you.

4. Listen more, talk less.

People relate to you well when they know you're paying attention to what they're saying. Don't talk over them and seek clarification before you craft a response.

**Treating others poorly**

Social anxiety makes you have tough days, from nervousness, fear, and panic to anger and frustration. Of course, with these feelings, you may find yourself mistreating others even when you don't intend to.

How would you tell you're treating others poorly?

- When you're aggressive toward them.

- When you make careless jokes that make them feel ashamed.
- When you become unapproachable— you're very volatile.

So, here's how you can stop treating people poorly:

*Don't look down on people.*

Treat everyone with respect. Whether someone is uneducated or unsuccessful, treat everyone with dignity.

*Be polite.*

Make requests, not demands. Use words like *"thank you"* and *"please"* when asking for something.

*Be sensitive to other people's feelings.*

For example, when you want to cancel a plan, say something like, *"I'm sorry I have to cancel, I understand it's disappointing, but I'll make it up to you soon."*

*Phrase your words positively.*

For example, instead of saying, "*I can't understand why you leave the washroom a mess,*" say, "*I wish we put some effort into cleaning the washroom daily.*"

**Being disrespectful to others**

Studies show that disrespectful teens are more likely to become disrespectful adults later.[2] This often happens when you are mean, insensitive, impolite, and inconsiderate towards people. Maybe you roll your eyes at others, backtalk them and stomp from the room—this could be interpreted as being disrespectful and also makes you highly unlikeable.

How to address disrespectful behavior:

*Apologize*: apologize when you do or say something wrong.

*Listen:* even if what you hear opposes your opinion, listen first, then calmly discuss your point of view.

*Pick your battles wisely*: if you've been in an

## CHALLENGE YOUR PERSONAL BEHAVIORS

argument that ended in disrespectful behavior, try not to do it again. Walk away.

**What impact do personal behaviors have on your life?**

Being a teenager is pretty close to being an adult. You start learning and showing independence in your teenage years. Unfortunately, your choices may not always sit well with your parents and the people around you.

Take doing drugs and taking alcohol or hanging out with the wrong crowd, for example. Those unacceptable behaviors ruin your life as a teen and block a successful life in the future. Even eating a lot of junk food harms your health. You gain a lot of weight, affecting you both physically and socially. It would be hard to shed that weight leading to social anxiety issues.

Understandably, it's hard to transition from negative personal behaviors to positive ones, but with practice and persistence, it's eventually doable.

**Is it your fault for behaving the way you do as a teen?**

Sometimes it isn't. It is a process of growth.

Studies show that a human brain doesn't develop fully until the mid or late twenties. And the part of your brain still under formation during your teenage years is responsible for decision-making, planning, and a higher level of thinking.[8]

Make no mistake; there are normal teen behaviors, and then there are those that aren't very normal behaviors. Being abusive, stealing, or coming home late are behaviors that are out of control. They need intervention and tools to help teens behave better. Besides the development aspect, a teenager's negative behavior may result from a family breakdown. The teen becomes bitter with the parents and people around.

**Can you challenge your behaviors?**

Of course, yes. Suppose you find yourself a support system (family and professionals), set your goals, have positive self-talk, and reward yourself. In that case, you're on the road to acquiring a new set of personal behaviors.

# CHAPTER 5
# CHOOSE CHANGE FOR YOUR THOUGHTS

What you think controls what you do and even how you do it. Someone wise once said,

*"If you think you can't, you won't. If you think you can, you will."*
— Linda Ward

But your thinking isn't set in stone. You can change it. Just like you can learn how to play chess or ride a bike, you can learn how to change your thoughts and control your life. Have you watched the movie *I, Robot*? Perhaps you remember where Detective Del Spooner pursued the robot, running away carrying a woman's handbag. To him, all he could make out of the robot running away with the handbag was that it had snatched it from someone. Little did he know that the robot was running to take an inhaler to its owner, the woman, who was asthmatic.[1]

You may have been in such a situation before. Maybe you've even looked back on your life and realized something you did and felt like crawling into a hole while wondering, "*What was I thinking?*" You might think, "*I was a loser in the interview.*" But a few days later, you receive a call offering you the same job you thought you wouldn't get. Those and many more scenarios are why you should choose change for your thoughts. You may think about something in one way, but it might have multiple interpretations. Here, I'm going to help you understand that you should change your thoughts. I'll also show you how that change shapes your life and how it can get you a desirable outcome.

## HOW THOUGHTS CAN HARM THE WAY YOU FEEL AND ACT

How you think about yourself automatically becomes your reality. You'll limit your capabilities if you keep drawing negative conclusions about what you cannot do and who you are. Research from the University of Louisville shows a link between behavior, feelings, and thoughts. What you think has a direct influence on how you act and feel. So, if you agree with the thought that you are a failure, you'll feel and see yourself as a failure.[2]

You might say, *"I'm not good enough to pursue my career further."* That thought makes you discouraged and not put more effort into your studies. Consequently, the lack of effort prevents you from working hard and reaching your full potential, and eventually, you miss out on finding a nice job. Or you'd say to yourself, *"I'm socially weird."* So, you stay in a corner by yourself when you're at a social gathering. And when no one talks to you, it reinforces your thought that you must be socially weird.

The good news? If you change your thoughts, you could change your life.

Here's how:

**Look for evidence**

Take note of those times when your thoughts were wrong. These thoughts will remind you that negative thoughts aren't always accurate.

**Challenge your thoughts**

Perform behavioral experiments. Test how true your thoughts are. Do what makes you feel worthy whenever you feel unworthy of doing something. You might see yourself as too frail to leave a comfort zone, but force yourself anyway. Get out and meet with people, join a club at school, or even go on a date. It might feel uncomfortable initially, but you'll start thinking differently with practice. Those self-limiting thoughts will begin to subside, allowing you to hit your full potential.

## HOW THOUGHTS CAN HAVE A POSITIVE IMPACT ON THE WAY YOU ACT AND FEEL

Would you rather be around someone who only sees the clouds or someone who sees the clouds and also sees the silver lining? Of course, the latter is better. Someone who sees the good part of life is more likely to bring you happiness and build your confidence. If your thoughts focus on the good part of things, then you'll always feel happy and act better. You'll even attract more friends who would love to hang around with you.

Here's how you can cultivate thoughts that positively impact your feelings and actions.

## CHOOSE CHANGE FOR YOUR THOUGHTS

First off, dig deep, and come up with thoughts related to the following:

- Your fears.
- Your insecurities.
- Things that frequently stress you.
- Your losses.

Then, write a positive, contradicting thought for every negative thought above. For example:

- If it's about fear of failure, think about that one event when you failed but still learned a valuable lesson.
- Insecure about your skills? Think about how happy you were when someone said you had done a great job.
- Your work may stress you, but think about how the same job brings joy to other people and helps them raise their families.
- If you've lost someone, think about the good times you had with them.

Practice this with other thoughts to shift your perspective to a more positive one.

## HOW THOUGHTS CAN IMPACT YOUR LIFE WHEN YOU ARE STRUGGLING WITH SOCIAL ANXIETY

I bet you've heard the adage that says, *"You are what you think you are, and the world is exactly what you think it is."* So if you perceive the world, other people, and yourself in a negative light, then that's what becomes your reality. And this is especially true if you're struggling with social anxiety. Social anxiety tends to color your thoughts with negativity, even when things are not the way you think they are. It can be difficult to think of life as other people without social anxiety think of it.

When you are socially anxious, you look at the world differently. You may look at:

- Strangers as people who are looking to harm you.
- Friends as being judgmental.
- People are generally unwelcoming.
- The world is somewhere you should avoid.
- Things will never improve or change.
- Your past defines your future.
- Opportunity as overwhelming challenges.

But chances are that these things will never

## CHOOSE CHANGE FOR YOUR THOUGHTS

happen. So you don't have to live with such thoughts. It would help if you changed your perspective and look at:

- Strangers as new friends.
- Friends as people who give you companionship and comfort.
- People as generally non-judgmental, welcoming, and friendly.
- The world is full of opportunities.
- Things will get better.
- Memories and mistakes as learning experiences.
- You have a purpose in life.
- Thankful that you have opportunities all around you.

Here are some practical tips to help shift your thoughts for the better:

**Change your self-talk**

The first thing you should do to have favorable thoughts is to improve your self-talk. Yes, those things you tell yourself in your mind. They can be your worst enemy or your best supporter. Instead of saying to yourself, "*I can't handle this,*" you can say it this way, *"I got this!"* Another way to improve your self-talk is to assume you're speaking to your best friend. Obviously, you cannot discourage your friend. You'll motivate and inspire them. Why not do that to yourself as well?

**Face your fears**

Social anxiety makes you fear failing, being judged, speaking in front of people, or rejection. Whatever your fears are, it's time to get over them. By conquering your fears, you'll have more confidence and positive thoughts.

**Practice gratitude**

Of course, you have something to be grateful for, even when you don't believe you do; your life, parents, siblings, health, name it. Gratitude is a sure way to change your thoughts and start seeing things from another perspective. Research supports this by saying showing appreciation cultivates a positive attitude toward life and leaves you feeling better and happier.[3]

## Leave your comfort zone

Sure, in your comfort zone, things seem easy. But that doesn't bring change or growth. Why? Because you're too familiar with everything around you and you're not open to new experiences, challenges, and opportunities. So when you leave your comfort zone, the only choice you'll have is to think through the challenges you'll be facing. As a result, your way of thought improves. And besides that, you'll build mental toughness and strength.

## Feed your thoughts with positive media

Read books, take courses, and attend shows and events to expand your knowledge, and you'll learn how to interpret different life scenarios. With consistent positive media, positivity will be on top of your thoughts. And the next problem you meet in your life, you'll solve it from a positive point of view.

### YOU ARE IN CHARGE OF YOUR THOUGHTS

Did you know that everything happening in your mind —all the sensations, feelings, and thoughts—is only happening to your inner world? Whatever you think isn't always the reality. Why, then, do we give so much power to our thoughts, especially the negative ones? Let's say, for example, you're doing a presentation in front of your class, and all attention is on you. Instead of focusing on the presentation before you, you'll start thinking about what your classmates will think of you —how they'll judge you negatively or laugh at you. Those classmates are not experiencing your thoughts at that particular moment. But you're about to let them do it when you start thinking about their perception of you.

When you show them fear, they'll think you have fear, might label you as afraid, and may even laugh at you.

Do you realize that the first thought only appeared within you? Your classmates knew nothing about it. Even more strange, you didn't have that thought in the first place. Instead, it just appeared within your awareness; you didn't choose it or even ask it to show up!

What if you didn't entertain that thought? Or engage with it? It already would have disappeared, right?

That shows that your thoughts only feel real if you fuel them with interest and attention. You're in control of your thoughts, and you can change them.

*Here are three steps to help you remain in charge of your thoughts:*

**Step 1:** Pause and breathe when an unwanted thought enters your head.

- Purposely stop and breathe in and out to relax your mind. This pause will clear your head and isolate the thought.

**Step 2:** Ask yourself, "Is this thought helpful?"

- If it's not and just bringing you anxiety, proceed with whatever you were doing.

**Step 3:** If the thought doesn't go away, replace it with something else.

- Our minds tend to focus on one thought at any particular time. Going back to our class presentation example, you can interrupt that thought by asking your classmates a random question. You'll be surprised at how quickly the thought will float away.

## SOCIAL ANXIETY AS A TEEN

Wouldn't it be awkward if people shared the same point of view? For sure, it would.

Suppose someone texts a friend, and the friend doesn't text back. What would different people think?

*Person 1*: They're on another call.
*Person 2:* They don't have an answer yet.
*Person 3:* They didn't see the text.
*Person 4:* They're busy.

Those are different answers from different people over the same issue. But these are probably non-anxious people.

Here's a point of view from an anxious teen:

*Reason 1:* They're avoiding me.
*Reason 2:* They don't like me (is there a way I can take the text back— here, anxiety is heating up).
*Reason 3*: I can't fit their circle.
*Reason 4:* They think I'm stupid.

But if you switch to good thoughts, you will rewire this negative thought pattern. Instead, you'll be happy with yourself and others.

How about changing your thoughts to more positive ones when dealing with a challenging thought next time? Try something such as:

- Is there another way I could do this?
- Could I focus on another thing instead?

With that in mind, consider changing your thoughts realistically and favorably.

## CHAPTER 6
## PRACTICAL TIPS

Your teenage years can be challenging, particularly for teens with social anxiety. Your body is constantly changing, and with it, your emotions. There are so many expectations for you to cope with and a lot of pressure to keep up with. You're building your identity, self-worth, and other relationships outside of close family members. You will doubt yourself at times and deal with overwhelming challenges, also. You will often have negative thoughts and self-judgments and may feel like you are suffering alone. But this couldn't be further from the truth. So many teens and people are dealing with the same challenges. After all, adolescence is hard. What if I told you, however, that there are practical, effective ways to deal with and overcome social anxiety and enjoy those seemingly challenging youthful years?

But you have to know that this won't happen overnight. Managing your anxiety successfully isn't a skill you'll learn over the weekend or overnight. I wish this were possible, but it's not. You have to be willing, able, and ready to put in the work and follow through. Start by opening yourself up to the challenge and be ready to do something about your anxiety. You don't have to accept it for what it is or give in to this reality. It would be best if you committed to overcoming your social anxiety; then, the practical tips discussed in this section will be extremely useful for you.

## PRIORITIZE MENTAL HEALTH

Think about this. When someone falls and breaks a bone, they are immediately rushed to the emergency room. No one tells them to walk it off, try not to think about it, or even that it's not that big of a deal. This is a good thing because the sooner that person gets medical attention, the higher their chances of making a quicker recovery. And this shows how much importance we place on our physical health and how much we value our bodies. The question is, why don't we prioritize mental health just as much? Why are there so many barriers preventing people from reaching out for help or supporting others in mental anguish? Sometimes, we find it easier to pretend like it's not happening—sweep things under the rug rather than deal with or confront them head-on. In the end, ignoring our mental health causes us more pain.

Mental health is the foundation of loving relationships and better physical and emotional health. If you don't prioritize your mental health and take care of it, your body, mind, and spiritual health will eventually suffer. Your mental health greatly impacts your feelings, actions, and behavior. For example, let's say you lose a loved one. You may think about that person a lot, which could lead to stress or depression. Your depression may then affect how you look at life, interact with loved ones, and think and feel about yourself and the people around you. For us to perform optimally and be the best person we can be, our mental health should be at its best too. Take care of yourself—physically, mentally, and emotionally first if you want to be a good friend, sibling, daughter, or son.

Give yourself the empathy and compassion you so freely give others. Create space for self-forgiveness, relaxation, and understanding to effectively avoid the stressors that come with those difficult teenage years. These changes should occur from the inside out because they will impact how you feel physically, mentally, and emotionally. Understand that having a clear mind will boost your self-esteem, body image perception, thoughts about yourself, and how you view situations that may cause you social anxiety.

How can you do this?

Be conscious about your inner voice. Your inner voice can be compelling, and you spend more time with it than with anyone else. But is that inner voice working for you or against you? Think about how you talk to yourself. Do you feed the negativity or positivity? When you give room for the negative thoughts to thrive, your mental health pays the ultimate price. Your mental health declines when you talk to yourself negatively, and this, as we have mentioned, affects your behavior, emotions, actions, and life.

If you went to your friend for advice or comfort and they blamed or accused you for everything that happened, telling you that it was all your fault, wouldn't it be shocking? But how come we give the same power to the negative voice inside our heads? Why do we put ourselves down, blame ourselves, or even tell ourselves that we aren't good enough? You are beautiful, smart, and talented. You have all it takes to overcome anxiety, make friends and excel in school. You can change your situation for the better and overcome your social anxiety. Start by telling yourself that you can do it. Take notice of that little voice and change it to a positive, encouraging one. Let it be your support rather than the voice that tears you down. Changing that inner voice and creating a positive shift in your self-talk will do wonders for your mental health.

Understand that it's okay not to be perfectly okay all the time. It's easier to pretend that you are okay sometimes—even to push back everything you feel to the back of your mind and distract yourself, so you don't think about your challenges. But it's okay to be anxious, stressed, sad, or upset. It's okay to admit that you are not okay. It's also okay to talk about what you feel; this is what it means to be human. No one expects you to be perfectly happy, normal, and okay 24/7. This is an unrealistic expectation. You'll be uncomfortable in certain situations, sad, overwhelmed, unhappy, or indifferent in others, and this is okay. Start by talking to someone about it and getting help and the proper support. This doesn't mean that something is wrong with you. Admitting that you aren't okay and seeking necessary help is the first step towards being okay again.

Take good care of yourself. The importance of self-care can never be understated. Taking care of yourself is instrumental in helping you prioritize your mental health. But you must understand that self-care is unique to every individual. What works for someone you know may not work for you. The best way to do this, therefore, is to find an activity, a game, or an exercise that makes you feel good and lifts your spirits. Hopefully, it's something that calms you, quietens your mind, and allows you to relax. When you engage in self-care activities, you are reminded that life doesn't revolve around the things that stress you or give you anxiety.

Do you love meditation, singing, the spa, or just spending time with family? Well, make time for these activities and put them in your schedule. Don't allow other things that seem more important to bump self-care activities out of your life continuously. I know that life goes by fast, and we have endless responsibilities, but this doesn't mean we shouldn't create time to love ourselves and care for our needs. For most people, this means taking care of themselves physically—eating a nutritious diet, exercising, and getting enough sleep. While all of this is good and, quite frankly, necessary, it shouldn't be all we do. The mind is just as vulnerable, if not more vulnerable than the body. Many of us neglect our mental health, but it's time we changed that. It's time to prioritize our mental health.

## SHIFT YOUR FOCUS AND REFRAME NEGATIVE THOUGHTS

Studies report that teens' brains are wired to focus on negative things and other bad stuff, like failing a test, a critical moment, or a missed opportunity, rather than all the positive things happening around them.[1] They will quickly forget the compliments they get, the good memories or the laughter they share with friends and loved ones, or a hug from someone they care about. This could explain where the negative teen stereotype comes from. Over time, the negativity leads to a negative attitude—anger, resentment, hopelessness, and severe mental health issues like depression and social anxiety. That's why you must reframe your thoughts if you want to overcome your social anxiety. Reframing your thoughts will quickly break the negativity you've held on to for too long and change your perception of the world and yourself into positive, more constructive thoughts.

But what is reframing?

Reframing, sometimes known as cognitive

restructuring, is an important building block of many therapy techniques. It is a foundational tool in Cognitive Behavioral Therapy (CBT)—a powerful therapy strategy that has proven effective in teenagers. According to this concept, our thoughts impact our feelings which then influence our actions. This means that your feelings and actions are more likely to change when you change your thoughts and behavior.[2]

For this reason, reframing can help you and other teenagers shift their thoughts and change their mindset and points of view so they can look at situations, people, and relationships from healthier and more positive perspectives. When you reframe your thoughts, your response to things happening around you will also change because you look at them differently. When you reframe your thoughts, you'll be able to:

- Look at the details of a situation from a positive rather than a negative perspective.
- Change your distorted thought patterns.
- Have a better comprehension of your experiences and analyze them objectively.
- Be aware of your thoughts and feelings.
- Question all the negative beliefs you have.

A negative outlook does nothing positive for our mental health. If anything, constant dwelling about what went wrong or what could go wrong undermines your well-being and emotional health.

Many teens lack self-compassion and empathy. They judge themselves harshly and imagine that this is what everybody else does. They put themselves down rather than be compassionate advocates of themselves. This is completely heartbreaking. One of the best ways to restructure your thoughts is to practice self-compassion and kindness. This can improve a teen's self-esteem and boost their self-confidence. Positive self-talk also trains a teenager's brain to appreciate the positive aspects of a situation rather than the more minor negative aspects.

For example, a teen can restructure their mind from "*I can never get this right, I am terrible at this*" to "*I am still learning to do this, and soon enough, I'll get it right.*" Or "*I ruined everything,*" to "*That didn't work the way I was hoping it would, but I know what I should do differently next time.*"

Experts believe the ABCDE method is one of the most effective cognitive restructuring techniques.[3]

*A:* *activating* event that starts the loop of negative thought patterns.

**B:** *beliefs* associated with the activating event, which often fuel negative emotions.

**C:** *consequences* or feelings associated with the activating events and the subsequent beliefs.

**D:** *disputing* and challenging the negative emotions and thoughts associated with the activating event and its subsequent beliefs.

**E:** *effecting* changes in your beliefs and feelings associated with the activating events and their subsequent negative emotions and beliefs.

So, how can you do this? Become more aware of your thoughts. Negative thought patterns are often so automatic and habitual that we don't realize we've made them our default setting. But when we are more aware of our thoughts, we will not jump to negative conclusions whenever something happens. We will learn to think about a situation before negatively branding it. We will notice our habits and tendencies and work towards changing them. If you want to reframe your thoughts, you must first recognize them.

Ask yourself questions. Try and use logical reasoning to challenge your thoughts and reframe them. Ask yourself some thought-provoking questions, such as, *"Is there another way to look at the situation?"* or *"Is there enough evidence to support my beliefs, or am I just encouraging negative thoughts?"* By analyzing the situation using thought-provoking questions, you may realize that you are overreacting or misinterpreting the situation.

Look at the bigger picture. Remember to look at the situation from multiple angles whenever you find yourself making negative assumptions and conclusions. For example, what you see as a failure could be an opportunity to learn something new when you look at it from a different angle.

Stay away from black-or-white thinking. Most teens look at things in extremes. Something or someone is either good or bad, right or wrong, nice or mean, and there are no gray areas—there are no in-betweens. Restructuring your mindset can help you overcome this thought pattern and understand that situations and people are not always as simple as you make them be. Every situation has a gray area, but you must look at it from that angle to see it.

Not everything is about you—so don't take everything personally. Teenagers tend to overthink and blame themselves for things outside their control. This isn't a good thing to do because it messes with your mental health. You must understand that so many things happening around you don't have anything to do with you. Some of them are beyond you, and the best you can do is accept the situation as it is. This way, you'll have peace of mind.

Learn to focus on the positive aspects of your life. Teens torture themselves endlessly by predicting and assuming what others think of them. They could look at a situation and think of its worst possible outcome. But if you learn to look at a situation positively rather than expecting the worst-case scenario, you'll be happier and more optimistic.

Shift your focus to think of more positive thoughts and reframe those negative thoughts altogether. These actions will help you develop a renewed mindset and focus on your life positively. If a person grew up in an environment where they viewed the world as dangerous, this would make them more anxious. How a person thinks must be refocused and reframed to replace anxious thinking with realistic and healthy thinking.

## CHANGE YOUR LIFESTYLE

Have you ever looked at or analyzed your life as it is and felt like you wanted to do something differently? Have you ever felt the need to improve in a particular area of your life? Maybe you want to be more active, eat healthier meals, move more, and overcome certain things you struggle with. Perhaps you need a lifestyle change—maybe you need to create new habits and stick to them. Perhaps through this, you'll improve your life and your situation.

I've heard what they say, "*Old habits die hard*," and this is true to a certain extent. Changing your lifestyle may include changing habits developed years ago and sticking to new ones you are trying to create. Changing your current lifestyle will not always be easy, and it could take a while until these new habits stick. Moreover, you may face challenges and roadblocks along the way, but the key here will be to make small changes with each day. These changes will become consistent and be seen in your life over time. They may also help minimize your social anxiety, as some lifestyle habits you are trying to change may have severely impacted this disorder in your life. Choosing healthy habits to work on is important, as this will manifest and play a massive role in your life.

Changing your lifestyle and adopting new hobbies and habits are good for your physical and mental health. Hobbies and new habits can help you overcome social anxiety, stress, and other health problems. For example, regular physical activity and healthier eating habits will help you stay within a healthy weight limit. You'll have more energy, and after a while, these habits will slowly become part of your daily routine.

Studies show that there are four stages of positive behavior and lifestyle change. Understanding these four stages of healthy behavior change will help you identify what you need to do to ensure your new habits lead to a change in your lifestyle.[4] The four stages are:

1. Contemplation & inspection
2. Preparation
3. Action
4. Maintenance of the habit

So what stage are you in, and what should you do about it?

**Contemplation**: "*I still need to think about this.*" You are still contemplating this change and:

- You are seriously considering the change but haven't gathered enough courage to start.
- You understand that developing new habits and sticking by them will improve your physical and mental health.
- You are still unsure how and if you'll overcome the obstacles that keep you from starting.

**Preparation**: *"I have decided to take action."*

At this point, you are seriously considering the lifestyle change and thinking of specific ideas that will work in your favor once you start. You are in the preparation stage if:

- You have decided to change.
- You are ready to take action.
- You have specific goals that you've set out to achieve.
- You are getting ready to get started.

**Action:** *"I am already making changes."*

You are acting on your desire to change your life

and actively doing what's required to create the habit. You are in the action stage if:

- The changes you've made are slowly filtering and becoming part of your routine.
- You have identified creative ways to stick to your new habits.
- You have dealt with challenges, clip-ups, and setbacks, but you've worked your way around them and made progress.

Once you've started acting and working around your challenges to stick to your habit, you'll also find creative ways to maintain it, and this will lead to positive lifestyle changes. The changes you adopt will become consistent and be seen in your life over time, minimizing social anxiety, as some of those lifestyle habits may have severely impacted this disorder in your life. Choosing healthy habits to work on is important, as this will manifest and play a massive role in your life.

## SURROUND YOURSELF WITH POSITIVE INFLUENCE

Do positive influences work? Does surrounding ourselves with positivity change us for the better? Studies show that positive influences are highly effective in positive behavioral change.[5] Whether you are trying to lose weight, maintain sobriety, or change your mindset, surrounding yourself with positive people has long-lasting effects on your life. Therefore, so much of your positive thoughts have a lot to do with whom you choose to surround yourself with. This isn't to say that you should be looking for the perfect people to spend time with—quite the contrary. It means you should find a company of people who encourage you to desire better for yourself—people who appreciate positivity. These people motivate you and cheer you on as you are trying to overcome your challenges, such as overcoming social anxiety. They give you emotional and even financial support when you need it and encourage you when you are overwhelmed with your struggles.

People who positively influence you aren't necessarily perfect or happy all the time. They don't have to be because no one is perfect or always happy. But these people are always trying their best to influence your life positively. They could be your schoolmates, siblings, family, or colleagues. You know they care for you and have your best interests at heart. They want to see you doing your best and accomplishing all your goals. Spending time with people who influence you positively makes it much easier to focus on your goals. You look at life with a new perspective and feel good about yourself and everything you've achieved.

And we all want to be happy and to thrive and be successful. But why do so few of us achieve this? The answer is simple—what are your standards? Who are you surrounding yourself with? Stay away from people who bring you down, and stay close to those who lift you up instead. Stick with people willing to share their knowledge with you, help you learn from your mistakes, and inspire you to do better. The goal is to raise your standard as it relates to your inner circle.

You've heard it before, "*You are a product of the people you hang around.*" That's because it is true. Those we spend time with, impact our moods, emotions, perceptions of the world, and opinions significantly. This is also known as the power of proximity. With positive people around you, you are more likely to adopt empowering beliefs and see life as something happening in your favor, not against you. Indeed, you benefit a lot by surrounding yourself with people who make you happy, but you suffer when people around you are narrow-minded and negative.

So, what kind of people influence you positively?

*Smart people:* make sure the people around you are smarter than you. Such people will push you to desire more learning and to stay curious about your world and everything happening around you. These are important habits of people who succeed later in life— they are always curious and learning.

*Hardworking people:* to overcome your challenges and succeed, you have to be more than smart. There are so many people out there who are extremely smart but have no desire to succeed and have, therefore, never succeeded. When you have a hard worker around, their hunger inspires you to put in just as much work or to do more to achieve your goals.

*Dreamers:* our world is full of doers, but it needs dreamers just as much. When you have a dreamer in your circle, you'll always be entertained with the wildest ideas and constantly be challenged to chase your dreams.

*Positive thinkers:* indeed, no one is happy every hour of every day, but some people look at their challenges not as obstacles but as opportunities for growth. While others see their challenges as insurmountable roadblocks, positive thinkers learn and grow from their challenges. When things get tough, you want to be surrounded by positive thinkers.

## FACE YOUR FEARS

Socially anxious teenagers feel uncomfortable in many settings. They would rather not raise their hand in class to ask a question, even when they have one. They avoid strangers and talking to people they don't know, ordering food, eating in public, or presenting in class. It doesn't have to be like this, though. It's normal to feel fear, but how you react to it determines whether or not you reach your full potential. You should learn to face your fears; if not, your fears will hold you back from achieving your goals and going for your dreams.

But why should you face your fears?

When you let fear take over your life, it keeps you from going after things you want to do. When this happens, you may miss out on important opportunities that lead to personal growth. When fear drives your life, it significantly limits your ability to thrive and grow. But when you face your fears, you'll realize that you are capable of greater and bigger things than you thought possible. Fear stands in your way of working on your higher levels of consciousness, such as courage, joy, acceptance, and self-love. Facing your fears, on the contrary, will help you achieve these things and reach your maximum potential.

Maybe you've been telling yourself that your fear will go away with time. Perhaps you've figured out different ways to work around it—you never raise your hand or answer a question in class, meet new people, talk or eat in public, or even say hello to strangers. But what you don't understand is that running away from your fears is nothing more than a band-aid fix—it works temporarily but never solves the underlying problem. For example, you avoid any public speaking situations because you are scared of people. This may work for a little while, but what happens when your professor needs you to do a class presentation or you finish school and have to make a presentation at work before your boss and the board?

## PRACTICAL TIPS

Will you escape these professional and academic responsibilities as well? Running away from things that scare you will only exhaust you. You'll be a victim of constant worry, but if you face your fears, you'll be free.

# CHAPTER 7
# APPLICATION IN YOUR CURRENT SITUATION

Many people dislike change because change is uncomfortable. But you'd be intrigued to learn that this is not entirely our fault. Studies show that the human brain is hard-wired to stick to what it knows. Yes, your brain likes to stick to what it knows —change takes time, effort, and hard work. Change is also accompanied by uncertainty, and the associated discomfort often throws people off from their sense of normalcy. For this reason, most people would rather stick to their comfort zone. As safe as the comfort zone is, it doesn't grow you, it doesn't challenge you, and it does nothing for your physical and mental health.

Therefore, you must find ways to shift your perspective on change. A positive shift in your mindset as it relates to how you perceive change

## APPLICATION IN YOUR CURRENT SITUATION

empowers you to embrace challenges and grow through the inevitable transitions in life. Change doesn't have to be uncomfortable—or at least we can learn to embrace this discomfort, knowing it leads to something beautiful. How you perceive change directly impacts your life because it determines how you cope with challenging situations. Start by saying yes to change and embracing said changes in your life by taking small steps each day. During this process, always remember that social anxiety does NOT define you as a person. This journey will be one that will take time, but the end will be rewarding, and you will see how much you've grown. When you accept and even embrace change, you give yourself endless opportunities to grow, learn new skills, improve your adaptability and flexibility, and be the best version of yourself as you move forward.

Understand that you are in charge of your behavior, thoughts, and actions as a teen. No one can take care of that but you. Take advantage of this fact and change your life for the better. Take advantage of the opportunities around you and improve your life and perspective. This section highlights different ways you can do this by applying the aforementioned five practical tips to your life.

## PRIORITIZE MENTAL HEALTH

> *"By taking care of myself, I have so much more to offer the world than I do when I am running on empty."*
> – Ali Washington

Prioritizing your mental health is more complex than it sounds. It is a process that takes continuous effort. In the same way that our bodies need exercise, rest, and nutritious foods to function optimally, our minds must be cared for in the same way to function well. So, how and where do you start taking care of your mental health?

**Speak kindly to yourself**

Imagine if someone told you, a friend or a sibling, for example, *"You look horrible in that outfit. It makes you look fat—I can literally see your stomach bulging from here."* Or *"You don't look so good, and your room is a complete mess. How can you be okay with such a messy space? Are you ever going to get your act together?"* How would any of these statements make you feel?

## APPLICATION IN YOUR CURRENT SITUATION

There are certain things none of us would ever want to hear from some of the most important people in our lives. Then why do we turn around and do the exact thing to ourselves? Why do we say the same things to ourselves if we never want someone to say them to us? Some of the most damaging things we hear about ourselves actually come from ourselves. We are expert judges of our own flaws and characters, quick to judge and point out things we aren't good at, all the things we are not, and all the mistakes we've ever made. Some of us spend so much time putting ourselves down and talking negatively that we don't even notice anymore. It's like negative self-talk has become our default setting. At some point, we convince ourselves so much that it sounds accurate—like that's the truth when, in reality, it's not.

And I'm sure you've wondered why we do this.

Well, we all have something called the inner critic. It's like a critic watching your life from the sidelines. They have a crystal-clear memory of everything you've been criticized, shamed, or bullied for. It remembers all the stressful and traumatic events you've been through, all the expectations people have of you, and the ones you have of yourself. Your inner critic acts as if they dislike you, but they are trying to protect you. Every time you do something your inner critic perceives as emotionally risky or threatening, they step in to "protect" you. They say whatever they need to, to keep you from rejection, failure, criticism, or disappointment.[1]

For example, let's say you are trying to make a change and eat healthier foods. Your inner critic worries that you could fail or slip up and end up with your regular junk. It's better if they could protect you from something that will lead to disappointment down the road. So, when you pass by your local fast-food joint, they say, *"Well, you might as well order your regular junk—you'll never stick to healthier food choices anyway. You've failed so many times before—maybe you should just quit trying already. Just do it; you already know this is how it will end, right?"*

Sadly, most of us give in to this kind of negative self-talk, not realizing it does more harm than good. This negative self-talk leads to hopelessness, low self-esteem, shame, and guilt. Negative self-talk is also linked to serious mental health issues, including depression, self-harm, and suicidal thoughts. As if that isn't bad enough, there is evidence pointing to the fact that the more you repeat these negative messages, the more your brain finds reasons to believe and support them. So, the more you tell yourself these

## APPLICATION IN YOUR CURRENT SITUATION

things, the more you believe them, even if they are false.

The old saying, "*If you are not going to say something nice, don't say anything at all,*" rings true, particularly regarding yourself. This phrase applies to your self-talk as well. If it's not something nice, don't say it, even to yourself. When you learn to speak to yourself kindly over time, you become more confident; you grow your self-belief, self-esteem, and happiness. This approach is much more beneficial and motivating for you. Ultimately, it works in your favor and is better for your mental health than being critical and putting yourself down.

What's more, when you entertain negative thought patterns, you are more likely to attract negative situations that reinforce the negativity within you. But when you have a positive mindset, you attract positive situations that enforce the positivity within you.

**Love your body**

Maybe there's something you wish you could change about your body. If only you could change this or remove that, you could love your body or be much happier. But the big question is, why do you even want to change your body? Why do you have that deep-seated desire to look different? Maybe you want other people to like you and think people will love and accept you more when you look a certain way. We've all been told, from a young age, that looking a certain way will bring us love, attention, approval, respect, and value. But this couldn't be further from reality. Looking a certain way won't make you happier than you already are. If it did, then all the fashion models and celebrities we look up to would be the happiest people on the planet, but we know this isn't the case.

You must learn to let go of the idea that you wouldn't be sad, unhappy, or face rejection if you looked different. Some of these things are beyond you and have nothing to do with your appearance. The more you process and internalize this concept, the less you'll be attached to conventional beauty standards, and the less you'll torture yourself about not looking a certain way. Real happiness and peace come from loving yourself for who you are—your body included.

This isn't to say that discrimination based on these things doesn't exist. If only this were the case, but that would be us living in denial. It's unfortunate, but these unrealistic beauty standards indeed exist. Still, you don't have to bend over backward to achieve these impossible beauty ideals that will never make you happier or feel better about who you are. Ask yourself, is your body the issue, or are the impossible beauty ideals imposed on you the problem?

Instead of trying to fit into a system that pits you against yourself, what if you change your mindset and adopt one that designates you to love yourself as you are? How about you appreciate yourself and value yourself as you are? What if you stopped trying to please others or fit into what society expects at your own expense?

**Do something that will make you feel confident**

One of the biggest obstacles that held me back from chasing my dreams when I was younger was my lack of confidence and fear of failure. I lacked the self-confidence that would help me overcome my fears. And this is something that many teenagers struggle with. But how can you overcome this fear? Well, you must start working on your confidence—and build it, one step at a time. In building your confidence, you'll learn to overcome your fears and chase your dreams fearlessly. Indeed, you will still have fear, but you'll be confident enough to know that you can overcome them—that you can beat your fears and come out victorious on the other side.

You may be wondering, "*Is my confidence in my control? Do I have the power to change it?*" The answer is a resounding YES! There is so much you can do to build your self-confidence. No, self-confidence isn't inherited or a rare trait in a few lucky individuals. Self-confidence is like a muscle—it can be built and strengthened. You may be convinced that you aren't smart, competent, or brave enough—but all these things can be changed. You can become a person worthy of respect and admiration, despite what you and everyone else think.

Start by taking control of your life by doing things that improve your self-image and skills. For example, start by grooming yourself. While this may sound obvious, random even, taking a shower, combing your hair, taking care of your nails, and putting on clean, nice clothes can boost your self-confidence, self-esteem, and body image. There are days when my moods went from 0-100 on a positive scale when I did this simple thing.

Stand tall. I might not be the person with the best posture in the room, so giving this kind of advice may sound hypocritical, but I know it works because I use it often. I always remind myself to stand tall and straight; I feel good about myself when I do that. I imagine there's a rope on top of my head pulling my

## APPLICATION IN YOUR CURRENT SITUATION

head up, and the rest of my body follows this "movement" and straightens itself accordingly. What's more, confident people are more attractive. This sounds like killing two birds with the same stone to me. Who wouldn't want that?

Build your skills and competence. How can you do this? Study. Practice. Repeat. No, you don't have to do it all at once, just small bits at a time. For example, if you are good with words, start writing more. Write in your journal, create a blog, write some short stories, then go into freelance writing. The more you practice, the more you refine that skill. Set aside a few minutes to practice and build your skills every other day. This is one of the most powerful ways to build your confidence.

Smile—simple but super effective. You'll feel better when you smile, which helps you appear and be kinder to others. It might be a trite one, but it has a powerful ripple effect on everyone around you. Smiling is a good investment in your energy and time.

Other things you could do to boost your confidence include:

- Exercise.
- Practice gratitude.
- Volunteer.

- Read—this is one of the best ways to empower yourself.
- Work on things you've been procrastinating on.
- Clean your room and your desk.
- Think positively—of yourself and others.
- Get to know yourself.
- Be a positive person.
- Be generous and kind.
- Always be prepared.
- Have goals and work towards them.
- Be a person with principles and live by them.

**Do not blame others for your well-being; it is your priority to focus on yourself first**

A few years ago, the World Health Organization started a thorough analysis of an epidemic they described as the "health epidemic of the 21st century". This "epidemic" was a rise in mental health issues such as depression, stress, anxiety, bipolar, and PTSD, among others.[2] How did this come to be?

Well, everyone is chasing something. Parents are chasing 80 hour work weeks and their side hustles while kids are chasing social media likes, friends, and

## APPLICATION IN YOUR CURRENT SITUATION

a good time. I am not the one to be telling you what to do if that's what you want to do. But you shouldn't blame anybody for the outcome either.

Understand that your general wellness is your priority and is a significant part of your general well-being. Taking care of yourself improves your well-being, school work, and relationship with everyone around you. When your well-being is compromised, your physical health suffers as well. You may find yourself dealing with physical disorders such as headaches, chest pains, and heartburn. You may also struggle with mental health problems like stress, forgetfulness, confusion, disorganization, trouble learning, difficulty making simple decisions, irritability, nervousness, etc.[3] The "cherry on top" here is reduced productivity and efficiency at school and work.

Indeed, your wellness needs are unique from those of everyone around you. For example, some people may not feel good if they don't exercise or eat healthy meals. Others may not feel great if they don't spend time with friends and family. Bookworms may only feel okay if they get some quiet alone time to read; you get the point. Think about the things that make you feel good—those that fuel and feed into your well-being, then carve out enough time to do those things. Seriously, include those things in your to-do list and ensure you do them like you would other important tasks.

## SHIFT YOUR FOCUS AND REFRAME NEGATIVE THOUGHTS

**Build habits to replace anxious thoughts with realistic and more positive ones**

So, what was the first thing you did when you woke up this morning? Did you grab your phone to check your socials? Did you go to the bathroom? Pray? Or make yourself a cup of coffee? Whatever it is you did, chances are that you do that every other day, following the same sequence without breaking the cycle. But why? Well, because that's how humans are. They are creatures of habit; all of us are. And our habits impact our lives significantly. They affect our level of success, the quality of our relationships, and our physical and mental health. Studies show that our tendencies toward the things we suffer from, such as social anxiety, are affected by our habits, but we are not always consciously aware.[4]

Indeed, habits are not easy to break. That's

## APPLICATION IN YOUR CURRENT SITUATION

because habits exist biologically, and most are encoded in our brains. This means that our brains have our habits on speed dial. By doing this, the brain has less work trying to think about what needs to be done, and we can, therefore, easily exist on autopilot.

Did you know scientists can tell your habits by examining your brain scans alone? Well, that's how powerful habits are. But there is good news. The brain is like an onion with layers. This is seen when you commit to new learnings; they are "placed" on top of the old ones. Yes, you can never eliminate a habit entirely because it's already encoded in the brain, but you can commit to new learnings that form new layers that override the old ones.[5]

Take advantage of this and build new habits that can override your anxious thoughts and replace them with positive ones. Start by tracking your thoughts. When you track your thoughts, you'll understand your thought patterns. How will you change your anxious thoughts if you don't increase your awareness and insight into how they work? What will these records look like? They may sound like, *"I'm scared to do a presentation in class." "What if they don't like me?" "I know something will go wrong." "I'm not sure what my purpose in life is."* When you have these thoughts written down, you can challenge them.

"*Is it true that something will go wrong? What if they like me?*" And even if you don't know your purpose in life yet, you still have time to figure that out, and it's okay not to know.

## Identify the thoughts that are causing anxiety or feelings of anxiety

Now that you know your thought patterns and the frequency, you can identify, track, and pinpoint your triggers. Here's where your records will come in handy because it helps show which incidents and events set off the negative thought loop that led to anxiety. Some common triggers are rejection, feeling ignored, having someone say something unkind to you, or fear of the unknown.

## Challenge those thoughts that are causing you anxiety or feelings of anxiety

So, you know you have negative thought patterns, and you know your triggers, but how will you use these to your advantage? You can use them to challenge your thoughts and to convert them from negative to positive ones. This is also known as thought conversion. No, it will not be easy, especially at first.

## APPLICATION IN YOUR CURRENT SITUATION

You may feel like you are lying to yourself or pretending to have the glass half full, but you must keep going. Thought conversion is a skill you must learn, just like all the other skills you have right now.

Fake it where necessary because the truth is this might take time. Furthermore, thinking positively may feel foreign to you, especially when you are so used to entertaining negative thoughts. Remember, also, that you are retraining your brain to think positively. Whenever you have a negative thought, stop immediately. Then challenge that thought with a positive one. Reframe and convert that thought.

This is what it could look like:

**Negative thought**: *"I'll fail this class anyway, so why bother reading?"*

**Positive thought**: *"I am not very good at this subject, but I've been making good progress, and I know I can do better than last time if I am prepared enough."*

The best way to get this to stick is to practice and repeat as much as possible. Use a journal where necessary and challenge your thoughts there. Create two separate columns; one for the negative thoughts that crop up in your mind and the other for how you challenge them. We have just one life to live, and it's too short to live it on edge, anxious that something might happen or someone may not like us. It's time to do better—for ourselves.

**Focus on building positive thought patterns**

Understand that positivity isn't about always being happy, cheerful, or smiling. There's more to it than that. Positivity has a lot to do with your overall perspective on life and your tendency to focus on the good and positive things in your life as well as other people's lives. Be intentional about this and start building positive thought patterns. Make positive thought patterns a habit. Never stop looking for the silver lining in every dark cloud; always make the best of a given situation.

But first, what does a positive mindset look like? There are many traits associated with positive thought patterns, including but not limited to the following:

*Optimism:* shows your willingness and openness to take a risk and make an effort even when it's unlikely that your efforts will pay off.

## APPLICATION IN YOUR CURRENT SITUATION

*Acceptance:* having the complex ability to understand that things may not always turn out the way we'd like or want them to, but accepting that there is always room for improvement.

*Resilience:* the ability to bounce back from challenging situations and overcome adversity, failure, and disappointment rather than giving up on the first obstacle.

*Gratitude:* consciously and actively appreciating life and everything it offers and looking for the good in every situation and people around us.

*Mindfulness:* building our focus and dedicating ourselves to conscious awareness of everything around us.

*Integrity:* prioritizing our principles, choosing to be honorable, honest, straightforward, and truthful, and standing courageously in that decision.

Not only do these traits build into your character

and motivate you to build positive thought patterns, but they also work in your favor in significant ways—being optimistic, accepting, loving, grateful, mindful, and honest in life will help you build and maintain a positive outlook on life.

So, how do these look in real life?

- It looks like accepting what you get and not throwing tantrums over it.
- Embracing the unexpected and appreciating it even when it's not what you wanted in the first place.
- Motivating people around you and encouraging them to embrace positivity.
- Using the power of a positive attitude and a smile to change the tone of a volatile situation.
- Being friendly to strangers.
- Picking yourself up and getting back up no matter how many times you fall.
- Learning from failure and mistakes.
- Being happy for other people's success and sharing that moment with them.
- Being happy and appreciating what you have, even when it's little.

- Accepting compliments and giving them out to others.
- Telling others that you know they did a great job.
- Making another person's day, even strangers—not just children because adults go through difficult things too.
- Not complaining all the time—complaining is a complete waste of time. Do something about it instead.
- Giving out more than you expect and not expecting something in return—careful with this one, though. You don't want people taking advantage of you.
- Stay true to yourself.

## CHANGE YOUR LIFESTYLE

**Be mindful of what you consume**

Your body is like a machine that is constantly working. It is continually shedding and replenishing, creating and destroying, storing and emptying, and keeping what's necessary while letting go of what's not. Our bodies are designed to let go of things that don't serve us. This could be in the food we eat, the media we consume, the company we keep, and the emotions we hold on to. And all of these things work concerning each other. For example, when you are going through a painful experience and holding on to negative emotions, your body struggles to keep up with its normal functions.

Feel your emotions if you must, process them, and then let them go. Always remember that you are what you eat, the things you think, what you do, and how you feel. Stay alert and aware of everything you consume—physically, spiritually, and emotionally. Your diet isn't limited to what you eat; it's everything you read, watch, and listen to, as well as everyone you surround yourself with, including the people you spend time with. Stay alert.

**Slowly incorporate exercise into your activities (this can look like walking, running, cycling, etc.)**

Incorporating exercises into your daily routine doesn't have to be difficult—in fact, it's easier than you think. Most of us are stuck in a sedentary rut even though we have the best intentions for ourselves and our bodies. I'm sure you already know that exercise has numerous benefits for your physical, emotional,

## APPLICATION IN YOUR CURRENT SITUATION

and mental health. It improves your energy levels, mood, and sleep. It boosts your self-esteem and self-confidence. It teaches you discipline and commitment, all while reducing your anxiety and levels of stress significantly.

What's more, detailed, life-changing exercises are just a click away. But if knowing how and why we should exercise was all it took, we would all be in excellent shape. We all know it takes more to make exercise a habit. You need a smart approach and the right mindset. Some practical concerns, such as health issues and a busy schedule, can create real obstacles to exercise, and this is understandable, but some of our biggest barriers are mental.

Maybe you don't have the confidence, and this stands in your way of making positive changes, or your motivation flames out faster than a lightning bolt, or you are the kind that gets easily discouraged. This is all too familiar for most of us. But there are ways you can incorporate exercise into your routine. There are ways to make it less intimidating or painful and instead make it more exciting, spontaneous, and fun. For example, let's say you hate exercising. What if I told you that most people share your sentiments? But if running on the treadmill isn't your idea of a fun time, you could find something you love. It could be dancing, stretching, or Zumba. You could also pair something you love with exercise. For example, you can take a walk through a beautiful nature trail or walk several laps through a bustling mall as you window shop. Bike with a friend to make it more exciting or listen to an uplifting podcast or your favorite music as you walk.

Let's say you are "too tired." Well, you'll be intrigued to learn that exercise is a powerful energy-boosting activity. As counterintuitive as it may sound, physical activity has been proven to boost energy levels significantly—in the long run. Regular exercise keeps you refreshed, alert, and energized. Or maybe "exercise is too painful or too difficult." You already know that without pain, there is no gain. I know this is an outdated cliché, but it's still true. But if you'd rather not do that, you can build your strength by cycling, swimming, dancing, walking, doing chores around the house, golfing, gardening, and running. All these are effective alternatives.

**Incorporate self-care (skincare, hair care, etc.)**

Self-care is about prioritizing your body and its needs. It's about listening to your body, checking in from time to time, intentionally listening in on your

## APPLICATION IN YOUR CURRENT SITUATION

thoughts, and challenging beliefs and the thought systems that aren't aligned with your goals in life. You may feel like you are up to this challenge, but understanding the importance of self-care is one thing; adopting it and incorporating it into your life is another. Taking the time to do something for yourself that will ultimately improve your life, particularly when there's already so much going on in the world beyond your control, can be difficult.

But there are practical ways to do it. Start by defining what self-care means to you. Everyone has a different interpretation of what self-care is. For one person, it could be going on a vacation and enjoying beautiful scenery without worrying about work. For another, it could be going to a spa and getting a special skin treatment infused with aromatherapy or reading a book quietly before bed. Whatever it is, make sure you find time to do it.

Create a routine that allows for quality sleep. Studies show that we need at least 7-9 hours of sleep for our bodies to recover fully. This could be more than what your late-night social medial scrolls allow, but rest is integral to a well-rounded self-care routine. You need enough sleep to maintain your physical and mental health. Sleep adds energy, productivity, efficiency, and quality to your physical and psychological health.

Self-care could also look like this:

- Eating a nutritious diet.
- Decluttering your space.
- Taking a break from everything and doing something you love, like going to the movies, visiting a friend, or hanging out with loved ones.
- Dance a little.
- Detoxing from social media.
- Take care of your gut health.
- Say no and mean it.
- Going on a self-care trip.
- Getting a pet—they love you unconditionally, and never judge you even when you feel bad about your mistakes, and are always willing and ready to listen.
- Cooking healthy meals and drinking plenty of water.
- Reading self-care books.
- Creating time for yourself and guarding it.
- Creating a self-care plan.
- Meditation—morning and evening.

## APPLICATION IN YOUR CURRENT SITUATION

- Creative hobbies—learning a new language, an instrument, etc.
- Watching the sunrise or sunset.
- Helping others and doing volunteer work.
- Writing in your journal, blog, etc.

## SURROUND YOURSELF WITH POSITIVE INFLUENCE

**A family that has your back**

"Family first."

There's a reason why people say this. Your family will always love you unconditionally. They care for you deeply, and you feel the same about them. Yes, you may not always see eye to eye, and that's okay. Honestly, you don't even have to. This makes sense, especially in your teenage years—you may find yourself fighting and disagreeing with them more often than you did before. These things will happen, that's a fact, but that doesn't mean you have a bad relationship with them or they don't love you. Remember, everyone has their own opinions, values, and ideas, and you don't need to have the same values as them to be loved.

For so many people I know, myself included,

family, will always be a safe space, a place where you can go whenever you need a shoulder to lean on or a friend to lend a helping hand. It's easier to approach a sibling or parent with a problem because you already know they will be there for you. Even when you don't get along with them (like in the case of an argument or a disagreement, for example), they'll still have your back. I've learned over the years that unconditional love also means unconditional care.

Genuine love and care come from people who love you without limits. Whenever you are in need, they'll be there for you. Even as you are reading this, you already know who you can go to and can't when in need. Family is one of those places where you will never be turned away. Keep them close, and keep these thoughts at the back of your mind whenever you need help. Even better if you can return the favor and always be there for people who'd never let you down.

**Friends that you know will love and support you**

The relationships we have in life are extremely important. Many of them help form the foundation of who we are as individuals. The people we surround ourselves with say a lot about our character. Our friends act like mirrors of the kind of people we are,

## APPLICATION IN YOUR CURRENT SITUATION

who we wish to become, who we care about, and the kind of people we'd like to identify with. It's not uncommon to get stuck in toxic friendships; we've all been there. Some people will act friendly to you, but they have a bad effect and influence on you. But when you find a true friend, they will genuinely care for you. They'll be there for you whenever you are in need, more like a second family to you. These friendships take little to uphold and maintain and feel just right.

These are the friends you should keep close to. Supportive friends understand you and your needs. They'll stick by you through thick and thin and be there for you in the good and bad times. Simple things such as fights and arguments will never break you up or come in the way of healthy communication. Instead, both of you will learn and grow from the misunderstanding and come out stronger than before.

They may not always agree with you—they don't have to, but they still care for you deeply. When someone tries to cross or hurt you, they'll stand up for you and defend you. They are loyal, trustworthy, and genuine. Never will you have to question where you stand in your friendship with them because they will frequently remind you how important you are to them. Supportive friends are one of the most important people in your life. It doesn't matter if you are neighbors or live thousands of miles apart. A genuinely supportive friendship that feels right and there is a sense of security, no matter the distance. Both of you know that you are loved, appreciated, valued, and validated in the relationship whether you talk frequently or not. These are the friends you keep.

**Classmates who you never knew but have seen from afar**

Starting conversations isn't your favorite cup of tea. As it is, you are reading this because you want to overcome your social anxiety. But you also want to make friends at school and get to know the classmates you never knew but only see from afar. You are in school to study, but that doesn't mean you don't want to get to know others and even create new friendships in school. But how can you do this if you are socially anxious?

Well, how about joining a club? Your school has different clubs and organizations you can join. Find one that you love. It could be an art club, dance, volunteering, swimming, etc. Better if you find one that allows you to interact with people while helping a good cause. You could also join a study group, and

## APPLICATION IN YOUR CURRENT SITUATION

while there, you'll have to interact with the members and talk through some schoolwork. This is an excellent way to get some work done while familiarizing yourself with your classmates.

You have a phone, and you are active on social media. How about using that to your advantage? What if you sent your classmate's friend requests on social platforms such as Facebook and Instagram? And there's an unexpected benefit to befriending your classmates on social platforms—it takes little effort to talk to them online because you aren't interacting with them face-to-face.

**Mentors that you trust**

You've heard it too many times. We all need mentors in our lives. Just like friends, mentors can guide and stand by you through life's bumps, twists, and turns. From the simplest things, such as whether or not you should get bangs, to complex things, like the best career path as it relates to your strengths and the best investments you should make. And mentors are just as important in your younger years as they are when you're older.

But first, who is a mentor? A mentor is there to guide, support, and give you feedback along with the tools you need to thrive. They are often people who've been down the same road you are now and are currently sharing their experience and expertise on what worked or didn't work for them. Understand that anyone can be a mentor—friends, family, siblings, or someone you met at a networking event. They don't have to be people you can only admire from a distance. They should be available, willing, and ready to help whenever you need them. Mentors are good because they provide the insight, context, and experiences you may have limited access to or may not even have. They help you "get unstuck" so you can keep the wheels on whatever you want to do to keep rolling.

So, what should you be looking for in a mentor? They must have relevant expertise and experience. So, let's say you want to join a swimming club and do it professionally; you must find someone who has done it before. Find someone who has swum professionally before, as they are more inclined to know the waters.

Your mentor must be enthusiastic and willing to share their experience. They must have the experience, but it's twice as important that they are willing to share it with you. They shouldn't hand over their knowledge begrudgingly, be manipulative or share their knowledge vaguely. They should be happy to spread the word. The best mentors help others not because they want to bask in the glory of their achievements but because they genuinely want someone else to benefit from their knowledge.

Most importantly, a good mentor has to be honest and willing to give direct and genuine feedback. They must be respectful but not afraid to give you tough love where necessary. They know how to give kind, constructive, and honest feedback even when it could hurt your feelings. You'll need someone who can call you out fearlessly when you mess around so you can make better decisions moving forward.

**Therapist, if you choose to see one**

Many people assume therapy is only for weaklings, but this isn't necessarily true. Even the most successful people on earth embrace therapy. Therapy, particularly psychotherapy, is an excellent tool for success. Therapy is one of those things that everyone should try at least at one point in their lives if they choose to.

Here's why:

From a young age, we've been conditioned to think that our internal thoughts and emotions shouldn't be discussed out loud. But this is, by far, one of the worst things you can do to yourself. Sweeping your emotions under the rug and not working through your internal issues can culminate in a lot of problems down the line. If you need numbers to convince you, look at the statistics on mental health issues. Depression is responsible for billions of dollars worth of lost man-hours every other year and is the leading cause of worldwide disability. So, this conversation isn't so much about choosing a therapist but about the benefits of having one.

The benefits of therapy are long-lasting, so you are not just working through things you are dealing with at the moment, but also developing the right tools to help you deal with new challenges down the road. The positive effects of therapy last and even grow over time because the work gets consolidated slowly as you continue therapy. This makes so much sense as it relates to positive influences because you'll use the tools you acquire in therapy as reflective lenses that help you think about, talk about and express your feelings about your internal emotions long after you've finished therapy. The idea of opening up to your therapist becomes an internalized concept so that self-therapy starts right where therapy stops. Medication might be necessary in some cases, but there's always a risk of relapse when it's discontinued. But the idea of getting down to the root cause of a problem, as it is with therapy, is one of the reasons why therapy coupled with medication is often the most effective approach. It is always advisable to check with your doctor or medical professional before taking any medication.

We all know that psychological distress can trigger physical distress. For example, when you are anxious, you may sweat, tremble, or have headaches, and your heart could start racing, among other things. These physical symptoms can be debilitating at times, but therapy can help you deal with those physical symptoms because it addresses the psychological aspect of your problems.

What's more, repressed symptoms don't just go away overnight. They come back to trouble you in the worst ways possible. When you don't talk about your issues, the unexpressed feelings and trauma you've bottled up pile up, only waiting for the right time to explode. If anything, repressed feelings only linger and fester—they are like a ticking time bomb that goes off sooner or later. Even if you don't end up with a full-on breakdown at some point, not processing your emotions fully leads to negative thought patterns that may spill over to other areas of your life.

If that's not enough, therapy has been proven to help give people a new perspective on others as well. With therapy, you get to understand yourself and the people around you. This is particularly important in your teenage years when you feel misunderstood or like it's you against the world. When we hold onto negative emotions without processing them, they become our default setting, so we can only see the world through that particular lens. We are always making assumptions, jumping to conclusions, and judging others. But therapy allows you to do a reality check by analyzing why a person could have said or done something. Without your cluttered assumptions, it's much easier to understand other people's perspectives and points of view.

**Find those who can hold you accountable for your actions**

We all need to be accountable and answerable for our words and actions. This is particularly true when it relates to the things we do daily—our morals, values, ethical standards, societal expectations, our expectations of ourselves, and those of people around us act as the perfect accountability check-ins. Besides, our

## APPLICATION IN YOUR CURRENT SITUATION

family, friends, classmates, and sometimes strangers also push us to take accountability for our actions often. But it is also important to call in reinforcement where necessary. If you bring someone else, you increase the odds that you'll hold yourself accountable. When you have an accountability partner, you'll not let go of your goals easily because you already know someone is watching, ready to call you on it.

A good accountability partner should be willing and ready to support your desires for growth. They should know where you are currently, where you want to go, the resources available to support this, and in what time frame you want to get there. Your accountability partner must be focused, dedicated to your goals as much as you are, honest, trustworthy, and respectful. They could be your mentor, a colleague, a family member, or someone with the same goals as you. You also have a responsibility in this—you have to be respectful of your accountability partner. Only then you will be willing to take their constructive criticism and apply it to your life.

For mutual benefit, you could become that person's accountability partner too. This way, both of you commit to a common cause and pursue it relentlessly.

## FACE YOUR FEARS

It was much easier for us to face our fears when we were younger. We could look under the bed or inside the closet and see that there were no monsters there. But as we grow older, facing our fears is no longer as straightforward as it was back in the day. Now, your fears are so complex that you find yourself avoiding situations and people that scare you. No one wants to walk directly and willingly into a painful or stressful experience. Except when you continually avoid these situations, you become a hostage to that monster. This often involves hiding away from the stressors that make you uncomfortable and engaging in endless distractions instead.

Alas! As you do this, you are also avoiding challenges that will grow you and bring you joy. What's more, how long will you hide from your fears? You can't do this forever. It will strike you at some point, no matter how much you try to suppress it. And the likelihood that it hits when you need that emotional equanimity the most is exceptionally high. Fortunately, you can face your fears and even overcome them. How about you confront the bogeyman instead of pushing it away into a distant compartment of your brain and trying to forget about it? When you face it,

## APPLICATION IN YOUR CURRENT SITUATION

it loses its ability to rule your life and dictate your decisions.

So, how about you challenge yourself to:

- Volunteer in class.
- Speak to a new classmate.
- Offer to hang out with friends.
- Eat out in public.
- Order food by yourself.
- Have a small conversation with your teacher.
- Share a highlight of your week with others.
- Join building block groups that will help with relationship growth.

## CHAPTER 8
## LIVING LIFE TO THE FULLEST

Hopefully, by now, you understand that social anxiety can make your daily life extra challenging. For example, you may feel scared and more self-conscious than others, especially in social settings. You might fear mingling with people due to issues like low self-esteem. This fear could prevent you from living life to the fullest. You might have noticed that you don't just snap out of social anxiety. It takes time to outgrow it. There is the time taken to go through therapy and sometimes even medication. Such things and many others tied to social anxiety could also deter you from living your life to the fullest.

Living your life to the fullest isn't just about going out for a party or hanging out with friends. It's about living without limitations or fear—a life with a new mindset. Because the moment you let self-doubt and anxiety creep up your mind, you stop enjoying your life. Every day, you make decisions about your life; where to go, what to do, and more. So, you can decide what your daily routine will look like and how you'll have fun. For example, you can scroll through social platforms like Instagram to see people enjoying themselves. You can get involved and have fun. You could also check out YouTube, watch people do some trick shots and pranks, and even go ahead and do them yourself.

But this doesn't necessarily mean your days will always be cheery and bright. Of course, you'll have some bad days. But you must make the best of each day to be happy. As a teen, you sometimes feel overwhelmed with your relationships, school pressure, and other life commitments. And that's understandable. But to live life to the fullest, you can't keep complaining about these things. Instead, know what you want and get it without hesitancy or fear. Your most significant commitment should be to ignore limitations, face your fears, and find joy in your life.

In this chapter, I'll show you how to live your life to the fullest.

## EMBRACE DISCOMFORT

While there is nothing glamorous in facing discomfort and embracing it, learning how to persevere can teach you that you're strong enough to learn something from your challenges. Persevering and embracing discomfort gives you a deeper understanding of yourself, so you stay in the knowledge that every feeling you have (even the bad ones) is temporary, normal, and tolerable. This understanding will not only help you cope with your emotions, but it will also teach you that life is complex—and that's okay.

Here's how to embrace discomfort and enjoy your life:

**Understand that it's alright to make mistakes**

It would help if you understood that confidence, resilience, and learning are only achievable when you accept that making a mistake in life is okay. You'll do things imperfectly, slower, and make mistakes you could avoid. But mistakes contribute heavily to learning.

**Negative feelings are normal**

Negative feelings aren't fun, and they don't feel so good. But understand that they're normal and okay. They will eventually pass. As human beings, we have a range of good and bad emotions. And they are all critical. They help guide you through life and protect you from possible harm. They tell your body when to reflect, step back, and heal. While some feelings are uncomfortable, they're valid and come with a reason. Your work is not to ignore your harsh feelings, but to feel, understand, and process them healthily so you may eventually learn from them and give your body what it needs.

**Tolerate these feelings**

Even though you experience discomfort, be assured that you'll bounce back from it. Don't rush to remove an uncomfortable feeling. Instead, close your eyes, and sit in the fear, sadness, worry, or even pain. Listen to it, and then figure out how to grow from it.

**Manage the discomfort**

It would help if you did something about the discomfort. It could be a physical activity or talking to somebody. It could also be a mindful meditation or a distraction. Just think of something you can do to grow yourself positively.

**Tip:** There is always a reason why you feel discomfort and unhappiness. Sometimes it's because of things you can control, and other times things you cannot. But it's always helpful to avoid anxiety-inducing things or situations (as discussed in the preceding chapters). Learning how to control your entire stress levels and avoiding anxiety triggers can help reduce the intensity of anxiety and help you live a fulfilling life. Plus, you'll not have to cope with unnecessary discomfort.

Why should you try to build healthy habits and live your life to the fullest?

**You'll feel better about yourself**

You'll understand that the solution to social anxiety is to do the direct opposite of your instincts. You'll relax and get the pressure off yourself. You'll no longer struggle to be perfect. Neither will you try to change who you are to please others—you'll relax and be yourself. As you practice those healthy habits, your anxiety will continue to drop. And you'll begin to re-evaluate your beliefs and attitudes toward things. Gradually, your life will change for the better. When you embrace your life and overcome social anxiety, you'll fear strangers, teachers at school, or your schoolmates no more. You'll feel more comfortable contributing to classwork, such as doing class presentations and building new friendships with people around you. Moreover, you'll overcome the terrible self-destroying habit of looking for faults in everything you do and then putting yourself down for them. Instead, when you make mistakes, you'll not get upset anymore. The act of not beating yourself up will allow an enormously positive change in your life.

**Positive thinking**

Another breakthrough you'll have with good habits is having a positive view of issues. When you approach a situation or issue where you might feel anxious, you may say, *"This situation is not as bad as I see it in my mind." "I am only blowing the significance of this situation out of proportion. It's true; this situation brings me some anxiety, but I will employ my anxiety-coping techniques. The event will turn out to be better than I thought. And when it's over, I'll be happy I did it. I have been in such a situation before, and I made it, and even in this one, I'll do it again."*

**Socializing becomes easier**

With a habit like positive behavioral exercise where you introduce yourself to other people and talk a bit about yourself, you'll be able to interact with your friends freely at school or in a social setting. Although it can be nerve-racking, with time and repetition of the exercise, you'll make a lot of progress in this area. Imagine yourself being able to dance in front of your friends (something you couldn't do before). Isn't that fun?

## FIND HAPPINESS AND LIVE LIFE TO THE FULLEST

**Find and engage in activities that bring you joy**

We all wish to be happy. But sometimes, we tie joy to things happening around us and our circumstances. We look at happiness as something beyond our control. Well, it's easy to think that way and link happiness to the situation we're going through, for example, social anxiety. You might think, *"If only life*

## LIVING LIFE TO THE FULLEST

*was different, if only I weren't anxious, then I'd be happy and enjoy my life."*

But that's not how happiness works. Happiness should come from within, not from the things happening around you. Rise above your circumstances and learn to be happy despite what you are going through. This isn't to say that you'll always be happy, but you shouldn't base your happiness on external factors.

Try to engage in activities that bring you joy because they will help lift your spirits. Activities such as:

- **Playing board games**

You may have loved games like Chutes and Ladders, Connect 4, and Sorry! when you were younger. But now, as a teenager, your brain needs more brain stimulation—because you are growing older. You may play these games at times, but if you want to spend little time on the screen, you should look for board games that allow you to think more and make decisions. Scrabble, Monopoly, Ticket to Ride, Catan, Mancala, Phase 10, and Uno, among others, are all fun-filled games.

- **Attending a game**

If you have a keen interest in watching sporting activities and spend a lot of time watching soccer or baseball on TV, you can watch them during a live match playing in your hometown. It could be either an inter-school game or a bigger one. If you attend these live games, you'll interact with the spectators and players and revel in the excitement. It will not only be a life-changing experience but a very entertaining one.

- **Swimming**

Swimming is an activity that will take you out of your room and make you happy. You can practice different strokes or styles. Even more fun, you can experiment with diving too! Once you are well prepared, you can invite your friends and hold a pool party where you'll show off your diving skills and fantastic swimming techniques.

- **Biking**

Biking is an activity that will take you out of the house too. You can do it with friends, or you can bike alone and still have lots of fun! You can challenge yourself to visit a particular place or ride a specific distance. It's a great activity to exercise, go outdoors, and get some fresh air. Besides, you can take this chance to learn traffic rules and explore new places with your friends.

- **Photography**

Photography is a great way to train your mind to think outside the box. With it, you'll see things you see daily but now from a different angle. Nowadays, mobile phones have some good cameras. But you can still ask your parents to buy you a better camera for good picture quality. You'll be motivated to take more pictures and enjoy the outside world.

- **Spending time with friends**

When you spend time with your friends, you'll feel a sense of belonging and acceptance. Once this happens, you'll develop a habit of caring, empathy, and compassion. These important values help you feel good about yourself and life, making you happier. Spending time with loved ones is just as good for your mental health too.

One way to successfully carve out some time for your friends is by finding common goals you have with them. Spend time with them working towards reaching those goals. Accomplishing two or more things together is easier and more fun. For example, you can work out together, walk your pets together, try new things together, or even do your school assignments together. You could also find special occasions to be with your friends, like celebrating birthdays.

- **Bowling**

Bowling is a popular game for family nights. If you cannot go outside, innovate the game at home. Assemble some 'pins.' You can make these 'pins' out of some household items. Be innovative and use different items every time. Plastic bottles are more popular, but you can also use balls and soft toys as bowling pins. Use cardboard boxes, balls, or cushions as balls. See? You can start bowling right away from home.

- **Having a movie night**

Again, if you cannot go out to the movies, get

some of your favorite movies and organize a movie night with your friends or family. Discuss the movies you watch with them. Ask them what they think; could the movie have changed if the directors did certain things? Ask your friends to dress like the actors in the movie. Replay the movie now, trying to fix areas that you thought could've made the movie more entertaining.

- **Visiting the museum**

Absorb your culture by paying a visit to your local museum. You might have overlooked those local attractions, but if you visit them and be innovative, you'll find how fun they can be. Please take a few pictures, share them on social media, and tell the whole world about the place.

Why not organize a scavenger hunt if you have a flair for laying clues and puzzles? Let the players compete to see who obtains the highest number of items from a list you've created from the museum. Make prizes for the winners—and the losers too!

- **Attending a live concert**

You cannot miss this gig! The vibe, excitement,

and happy feeling of listening and seeing your favorite artist perform live on stage would make a lasting memory. Having a photoshoot and selfies of your joyous moments with your friends and the artist is a classy must-do activity! What about getting the musician's autograph? Nothing beats that feeling.

- **Doing a trampoline flip**

You jumped on a trampoline when you were a kid. There's no harm in doing it when you're a teen. You can have more fun with it by learning how to do a flip. Hang out at your nearby trampoline park or ask your parents to get one added in the backyard (it's easier than ever nowadays).

- **Camping in the backyard**

Camping is an excellent way to break the routine of your school work and connect with nature. A trip to scenic places like the mountains with family and friends would be fun. If not, get creative and camp in your backyard. Just pitch a tent, bring some blankets and pillows, set a fireplace (for your roasted cinnamon rolls, bacon on a stick, and other snacks), and you're good to go!

Being a teen is about enjoying some fun activities and places and living your life to the fullest while getting ready for the upcoming adult life. While there is a lot you might face at this stage, near and far, you don't have to make your life boring and get engulfed in social anxiety. After all, we all have one life to live —just one!

- **Spending time with family**

Spending time with your family is one of the best ways to foster happiness and create memorable experiences. It is especially true when you have siblings. Because with your brothers and sisters, you already have a good connection, and it's easier to start spending a lot more time with them. Having dinner with your parents and siblings at the table would be great in the evening. Or playing a board game after dinner would also be a good start. If your family doesn't consider playing games a good idea for having some happy moments, try outside activities— maybe a walk in the park.

Did you know that projects in your house can be an excellent way to get every family member involved and spend some happy times while still working towards a goal? Look out for projects in or around the house that everybody would be interested in, for example, painting the house or lawn mowing. Working together as a family will help balance everyone's weaknesses and strengths and bring everybody closer together. And this would be one great happy family, won't it?

- **Getting a pet that you can care for**

If you've ever had a dog as your pet, you can attest that a dog is a creature of habit. It loves to take meals at the same time every day and always expects its evening walk. So having a pet in your life brings a particular structure to your life and could be helpful for your emotional health and wellness. This routine around your pet's exercise and feeding habits can bring structure to your life and boost your mental health.

Having a pet makes you feel needed. It brings a certain degree of companionship that fills the void of isolation and loneliness. Your pet will love you with its whole heart and will want nothing in return. Nothing is more fulfilling than being greeted at your door after school by a wagging tail and a furry face! Your pet will never be disappointed in you and will never judge you. All it will ask is that you return the unconditional love it offers. Such a source of love without conditions can reduce anxiety and relieve stress.

Hopefully, you know very well that sometimes animals are prescribed to people for emotional support. Beyond that, having a pet can foster responsibility, empathy, and compassion. This contentment, besides being a significant element in the healing process of social anxiety, of course, helps you live a fulfilling life.

- **Reading a good book**

Nothing is as fulfilling as leaving your world and entering a utopian world. If you already love reading, you can start reading new genres and different formats. You can set up a reading challenge with your friends or family. Set up a challenge to see who completes reading a particular book first. You could also set up discussions and debates on the selected book. You could also try some reading games.

The beauty of reading an excellent book is exploring your imagination. You fill in the gaps you find in the book you are reading in whichever way you want—as long as the imagination makes you feel better. Not only that, when you are reading fiction, you escape to a different world. A world that is better than reality and a lot more exciting and fun than your own—a world where amazing stories unfold. Better yet, the freedom of reading a nice book lets you choose a world you'd love to get immersed in, lost in, and happy in.

Believe it or not, happiness and stress have a powerful connection. A stress-filled life is not a happy life, meaning reducing or eliminating stress can make you happier. Reading has some sound effects on your stress levels. Reading for as little as six to ten minutes brings down stress. And because you may not always afford to visit the Caribbean Islands whenever stress creeps up on you, it's good news that reading a good book has much the same results on your stress levels. So, regardless of your specific needs to be happy and feel better, there is at least a good book out there that can meet those needs temporarily.

- **Listening to music**

Whether you are frustrated or angry, cheerful or happy, anxious or sad, when you listen to some music, it transports you to a happier place. There's just something special about musical notes. Music lifts your spirits and calms your soul. Have you ever noticed that good music is like an all-inclusive, universal language? Isn't that fascinating? If the music is good, it doesn't matter what the language is. You may not understand the lyrics, but the music itself never seems too strange, and you can still enjoy it.

Music can also distress you and calm down your nerves. Meditative and slower tunes can help lower your stress levels and improve relaxation. But it's different for people because some like loud music to tune up their world while others prefer calm music. Fast tempos can physiologically and psychologically arouse you, helping energize you for the day. Set up a competition at home or something closer to that. Do this with your friends. Make the experience more entertaining by singing to your favorite artist's music. Sing your heart out as loud as you can. As you sing along, make some dance moves—this will put you in good spirits.

You can enroll in professional training to acquire many different dance moves. Just moving your body along to the music is enough to relax. *Serotonin* and *dopamine*, the happy or feel-good hormones in your body, are released every moment you make a dance move. This mechanism leads to general mental well-being and a good mood.[1]

- **Traveling somewhere**

Breaking your routine and traveling somewhere gives you a high chance of increasing your happiness levels. Your mental well-being improves when you experience new places, cultures, and people. Nothing leaves you happier than leaving your comfort zone, facing your fears, and defeating them. Being in a new environment, around new people and unique cultures, and fitting in helps you believe in yourself and your adaptation skills. You'll always be enthusiastic about visiting other places regardless of the hardships. There's nothing as fulfilling as that. If you reside in a busy city, you might have seen how difficult it can be to interact with people. Everyone is in a hurry. For this reason, your social circle may be made up of schoolmates and family only. But if you travel frequently, you can easily have many people to interact with.

While on travel, people may be interested in talking to you. Locals will be more curious to know where you come from, and that way, you'll kick off a conversation. While in your hotel or other popular sites, you'll interact with and meet other tourists from many parts of the world. These interactions will open you up and change your perception of the world.

Talking with people from different environments and cultures makes life interesting. Moreover, you'll learn a lot and shift your negative perception of life to a better one.

And because you'll likely travel with friends and family, the relationship with these people will become more positive and closer. Such healthy relationships evoke feelings of peacefulness, satisfaction, and happiness. You'll share those traveling experiences and create lasting memories. Such a connection works wonders for your happiness!

So, what does a life without social anxiety feel like, generally?

A life without social anxiety is a liberation from actively looking to belong to a group of friends and pursuing acceptance. It is about finding peace with yourself, what you are about, and who you are. It's about dropping pre-determined expectations that never seem to work for you. Ultimately, it is a life full of genuine confidence, self-love, and appreciation for everything life has to offer.

## CONCLUSION

Research indicates a constant, upward rise in teenagers suffering from social anxiety, particularly in recent years. Why is this happening? Well, Chapter 2 highlights some of the biggest triggers of social anxiety in teens. The emergence of social media, for example, and the pressures of living in the digital era, have exposed the younger generations to more anxiety than before. There is an underlying desire for perfection among teens. There is also a constant comparison between them, and these two are well-known anxiety triggers. In a world where most people are glued to their gadgets instead of prioritizing real-time connections and enjoying the relationships we have, there's bound to be trouble. The dramatic rise in teen anxiety over the last few years reflects how much our society has changed.[1]

CONCLUSION

Still, we can't blame everything on social media. The reality is that it's practically impossible to prevent social anxiety completely. That's because other factors beyond our control are known to cause or aggravate social anxiety—I'm talking about biological factors, environmental factors, and life experiences, among other things. But we've also come to understand that avoidance can worsen social anxiety in the long run. For this reason, it's crucial that teens seek support and that parents support their anxious teens. What can a parent do? They can start by validating their child's experiences, knowing that what they are going through is real. They can then encourage them to face their fears, choose change for their thoughts and challenge their behaviors, as highlighted in chapters 5, 6, and 7. By doing this, parents can help children deal with and reduce their social anxiety while building their confidence.

And now we know that not seeking help soon enough for social anxiety may lead to more complex issues for both the parent and the teens down the road. As you go through chapter 3, you'll realize that social anxiety can particularly lead to isolation, which could impact a teen's relationships and ability to connect with family. The effects of social anxiety can also spill over to their schoolwork, particularly if they were to be put in the spotlight, like being called out in class or asked to do a presentation. They'll struggle to build or maintain friendships, especially when they realize that it's possible to reduce the effects of social anxiety by avoiding social situations. Lack of self-esteem is a genuine concern because one of the biggest components of social anxiety is an extreme fear of being negatively judged by others.

Fortunately, we can all build confidence and overcome social anxiety. Overcoming social anxiety can be life-changing. You'll be more confident in social situations, and you can build your self-worth and self-esteem. Simple tasks, such as asking for help at the grocery store or a question in class, become just that —simple.

This book lays out simple yet effective strategies to overcome anxiety throughout the last three chapters. You have it in you to overcome social anxiety. Read those chapters keenly and practice what they teach. Soon enough, you'll slowly notice that initiating conversations with your friends or strangers isn't as threatening as it seems. You'll have no fear of being judged or perceived negatively. Yes, you'll probably still feel nervous, but you'll know that the feeling is temporary and fleeting.

What's more, your social interactions won't

## CONCLUSION

impact your life as they did before. You'll be confident in your ability to thrive in social settings so you can slowly gain independence and create healthy connections with people around you. And the best part is that this book will always be your best guide in overcoming social anxiety. The strategies in this book helped me overcome my anxiety, so I am confident you'll overcome yours, too—sooner or later, but preferably sooner. You have it all in here; just put it to use and watch your life transform right in front of your eyes. I wish you the best as you start working on yourself.

I also hope you found this book helpful and valuable. If you did, please submit an honest and genuine review to the platform you obtained this copy from. This way, others get to read them and see this as a guide that can help them in the same way it has you and me.

Thank you.

Your friend,

*Natasha Rae Simmons*

# REFERENCES

**Introduction:**
1. *Any anxiety disorder.* (n.d.). National Institute of Mental Health. https://www.nimh.nih.gov/health/statistics/any-anxiety-disorder

**Chapter 1:**
1. Holland, K. (2023). *Everything you need to know about anxiety.* Healthline. https://www.healthline.com/health/anxiety-complications
2. *Any anxiety disorder.* (n.d.). National Institute of Mental Health. https://www.nimh.nih.gov/health/statistics/any-anxiety-disorder

**Chapter 2:**
1. Dekin, S. (2021). *Teenage anxiety on the rise: What's contributing to this problem?* Mission Harbor Behavioral Health. https://sbtreatment.com/blog/teenage-anxiety-on-the-rise-whats-contributing-to-this-problem
2. The Recovery Village. (2022). *Anxiety disorders facts and statistics.* The Recovery Village. https://www.therecoveryvillage.com/mental-health/anxiety/anxiety-disorder-statistics
3. Cuncic, A. (2020). *Social anxiety disorder in children.* Verywell Mind. https://www.verywellmind.com/bullying-effects-social-anxiety-child-3024250
4. Vassar, G. (2022). *What is the impact of child abuse on teenagers?* Lakeside. https://lakesidelink.com/blog/what-is-the-impact-of-child-abuse-on-teenagers
5. Harness, J., & Javankbakht, A. (2021). *Trauma.* Anxiety & Depression Association of America. https://adaa.org/understanding-anxiety/trauma
6. Mayo Clinic Staff. (2018). *Anxiety disorders.* Mayo Clinic.

# REFERENCES

https://www.mayoclinic.org/diseases-conditions/anxiety/symptoms-causes/syc-20350961

7. *Does anxiety run in families?* (2020). UNC Health Talk. https://healthtalk.unchealthcare.org/does-anxiety-run-in-families
8. Cuncic, A. (2023). *Understanding the causes of social anxiety disorder.* Verywell Mind. https://www.verywellmind.com/social-anxiety-disorder-causes-3024749
9. Linsambarth, S., Moraga-Amaro, R., Qunitana-Donoso, D., Rojas, S., & Stehberg, J. (2017). *The amygdala and anxiety.* IntechOpen. https://www.intechopen.com/chapters/55211
10. Lu, W., Rainie, L., & Shin, I. (2015). *Psychological stress and social media use.* Pew Research Center. https://www.pewresearch.org/internet/2015/01/15/psychological-stress-and-social-media-use
11. Walsh, D. (2022). *Study: Social media use linked to decline in mental health.* MIT Management. https://mitsloan.mit.edu/ideas-made-to-matter/study-social-media-use-linked-to-decline-mental-health
12. Twenge, J. M. (2017). *Have smartphones destroyed a generation?* The Atlantic. https://www.theatlantic.com/magazine/archive/2017/09/has-the-smartphone-destroyed-a-generation/534198
13. Heitz, D. (2019). *Self-esteem.* Healthline. https://www.healthline.com/health-news/2-3-of-parents-say-their-kids-are-self-conscious-about-their-appearance
14. Graf, N., & Horowitz, J. M. (2019). *Most U.S. teens see anxiety and depression as a major problem among their peers.* Pew Research Center. https://www.pewresearch.org/social-trends/2019/02/20/most-u-s-teens-see-anxiety-and-depression-as-a-major-problem-among-their-peers
15. *Types of peer pressure.* (2021). AspenRidge Recovery.

# REFERENCES

https://www.aspenridgerecoverycenters.com/types-of-peer-pressure

16. Sparks, S. D. (2013). *Teenagers are wired for peer approval, study says*. EducationWeek. https://www.edweek.org/leadership/teenagers-are-wired-for-peer-approval-study-says/2013/05
17. Abdallah, E. S., Abdel-hady, R. F., El-Sheikh, M. S., & Elzeiny, H. H. (2016). Association between social phobia and parenting styles among secondary school students. *American Journal of Nursing Science, 5(3), 96-105*. https://doi.org/10.11648/j.ajns.20160503.14
18. Aktar, E., Bögels, S. M., De Vente, W., & Majdandžić, M. (2017). Parental expressions of anxiety and child temperament in toddlerhood jointly predict preschoolers' avoidance of novelty. *Journal of Clinical Child & Adolescent Psychology, 47(sup1), S421–S434*. https://doi.org/10.1080/15374416.2017.1371029
19. Fox, N. A., & Pine, D. S. (2012). *Temperament and the emergence of anxiety disorders*. National Library of Medicine. https://www.ncbi.nlm.nih.gov/pmc/articles/PMC3619214
20. Braich, A. S. (2021). *The link between social anxiety disorder and attachment theory*. Camino Recovery. https://www.caminorecovery.com/blog/the-link-between-social-anxiety-disorder-and-attachment-theory
21. Anderson, M. (2018). *A majority of teens have experienced some form of cyberbullying*. Pew Research Center. https://www.pewresearch.org/internet/2018/09/27/a-majority-of-teens-have-experienced-some-form-of-cyberbullying
22. Mayo Clinic Staff. (2021). *Social anxiety disorder (social phobia)*. Mayo Clinic. https://www.mayoclinic.org/diseases-conditions/social-anxiety-disorder/diagnosis-treatment/drc-20353567

**Chapter 3:**

1. D'Amico, P. (2024). *What to do about teen anxiety and school*

# REFERENCES

*refusal*. Paradigm Treatment. https://paradigmtreatment.com/teen-anxiety-school-refusal
2. D'Amico, P. (2015). *Why teen struggle staying true to themselves and fitting in*. Paradigm Treatment. https://paradigmtreatment.com/staying-true-to-yourself-and-the-struggle-of-fitting-in
3. *Anxiety disorders: Affecting Americans by the millions*. (2021). Lifeskills South Florida. https://www.lifeskillssouthflorida.com/mental-health-blog/anxiety-disorders-affecting-americans-by-the-millions

**Chapter 4:**
1. *WHO highlights urgent need to transform mental health and mental health care*. (2022). World Health Organization. https://www.who.int/news/item/17-06-2022-who-highlights-urgent-need-to-transform-mental-health-and-mental-health-care
2. Mayo Clinic Staff. (2022). *Exercise and stress: Get moving to manage stress*. Mayo Clinic. https://www.mayoclinic.org/healthy-lifestyle/stress-management/in-depth/exercise-and-stress/art-20044469
3. Lawson, K., & Towey, S. (n.d.). *Lifestyle Changes*. University of Minnesota. https://www.takingcharge.csh.umn.edu/what-lifestyle-changes-are-recommended-anxiety-and-depression
4. Centers for Disease Control and Prevention. (2024). *Risk and protective factors for suicide*. U.S. Department of Health and Human Services. https://www.hhs.gov/answers/mental-health-and-substance-abuse/does-alcohol-increase-risk-of-suicide/index.html
5. *Disrespectful behaviors: Their impact, why they arise and persist, and how to address them (part II)*. (2014). Institute of Safe Medication Practices. https://www.ismp.org/resources/disrespectful-behaviors-their-impact-why-they-arise-and-persist-and-how-address-them-part
6. *Drugs, brains, and behavior: The science of addiction*. (2020). National Institute on Drug Abuse. https://nida.nih.gov/publica-

# REFERENCES

tions/drugs-brains-behavior-science-addiction/treatment-recovery

7. Massarat, N., Gelles-Watnick, R., & Vogels, E. A. (2022). *Teens, social media and technology 2022*. Pew Research Center. https://www.pewresearch.org/internet/2022/08/10/teens-social-media-and-technology-2022

8. *The teen brain: 7 things to know*. (2023). National Institute of Mental Health. https://www.nimh.nih.gov/health/publications/the-teen-brain-7-things-to-know

**Chapter 5:**

1. Proyas, A. (Director). (2004). *I, Robot* [Film]. Davis Entertainment Company; Laurence Mark Productions; Mediastream IV; Overbrook Entertainment; Twentieth Century Fox.

2. *Thoughts, feelings and behaviours*. (n.d.). FutureLearn. https://www.futurelearn.com/info/courses/depression-young-people/0/steps/36858

3. Sakrani, F. (n.d.). *Attitude of gratitude*. Mind Chicago. https://mindchicago.com/articles/attitude-of-gratitude

**Chapter 6:**

1. *Teen brain: Behavior, problem solving, and decision making*. (2017). American Academy of Child & Adolescent Psychiatry. https://www.aacap.org/AACAP/Families_and_Youth/Facts_for_Families/FFF-Guide/The-Teen-Brain-Behavior-Problem-Solving-and-Decision-Making-095.aspx

2. Stanborough, R. J. (2023). *How to change negative thinking with cognitive restructuring*. Healthline. https://www.healthline.com/health/cognitive-restructuring

3. *The ABCDE coaching model: A simple summary*. (n.d.). World of Work Project. https://worldofwork.io/2019/06/abcde-coaching-model

4. *The stages of change*. (n.d.). Virginia Tech. https://www.cpe.vt.edu/gttc/presentations/8eStagesofChange.pdf

5. *What factors can affect behaviour?* (2020). NSW Government.

# REFERENCES

https://www.health.nsw.gov.au/mentalhealth/psychosocial/principles/Pages/behaviour-factors.aspx

**Chapter 7:**

1. *3 reasons your inner critic doesn't want to leave your mind.* (n.d.). Big Self School. https://www.bigselfschool.com/post/3-reasons-your-inner-critic-persists
2. Fink, G. (2016). *Stress: The health epidemic of the 21st century.* SciTech Connect. https://scitechconnect.elsevier.com/stress-health-epidemic-21st-century
3. Robinson, J. (2023). *How does mental health affect physical health?* WebMD. https://www.webmd.com/mental-health/how-does-mental-health-affect-physical-health
4. Dalio, R. (n.d.). *Choose your habits well.* Principles. https://www.principles.com/principles/e3617553-aed5-4ac8-a694-a9248130d9a0
5. Groopman, J. (2019). *Can brain science help us break bad habits?* The New Yorker. https://www.newyorker.com/magazine/2019/10/28/can-brain-science-help-us-break-bad-habits

**Chapter 8:**

1. Watson, S. (2024). *Feel-good hormones: How they affect your mind, mood, and body.* Harvard Health Publishing. https://www.health.harvard.edu/mind-and-mood/feel-good-hormones-how-they-affect-your-mind-mood-and-body

**Conclusion:**

1. *Teen brain: Behavior, problem solving, and decision making.* (2017). American Academy of Child & Adolescent Psychiatry. https://www.aacap.org/AACAP/Families_and_Youth/Facts_-for_Families/FFF-Guide/The-Teen-Brain-Behavior-Problem-Solving-and-Decision-Making-095.aspx

Printed in Dunstable, United Kingdom